THE HALL IN THE GARDEN

Freemasons' Hall and its Place in London

The Library and Museum of Freemasonry

THE HALL IN THE GARDEN
Freemasons' Hall and its Place in London

The Library and Museum of Freemasonry

First published 2006

ISBN (10) 0 85318 264 7
ISBN (13) 978 0 85318 264 1

All rights reserved. No part of this book may be reproduced or transmitted in any form or by any means, electronic or mechanical, including photocopying, recording or by any information storage and retrieval system, without permission from the Publisher in writing.

© The Library and Museum of Freemasonry 2006

Published by Lewis Masonic

an imprint of Ian Allan Publishing Ltd, Hersham, Surrey KT12 4RG.

Printed in England by Ian Allan Printing Ltd, Hersham, Surrey KT12 4RG.

Code:0607/B2

Visit the Ian Allan Publishing website at www.Lewismasonic.com

Front cover:
Freemasons' Hall from Long Acre

Back cover:
Watercolour of Freemasons' Tavern c1800

Picture credits:
Unless credited otherwise, all the pictures in this book are the copyright of The Library and Museum of Freemasonry

Contents

Acknowledgement and a note on measurement and money 3

Introduction 4

Great Queen Street and its Environs in the 18th Century 6

The First Freemasons' Hall 7

Paying for the Hall 12

The Impact of the Union 20

Furnishing the Hall 23

Great Queen Street and its Environs in the 19th century 33

The Victorian Freemasons' Hall 35

Freemasons' Tavern 44

Great Queen Street and its Environs in the 20th Century 49

The Library and Museum 55

The Masonic Million Memorial Fund 59

The Building at War 75

Great Queen Street after 1945 78

Freemasons' Hall: A Photographic Essay 81

Notes on Sources 96

Acknowledgement

The headquarters of English freemasonry have been located in Great Queen Street since the last quarter of the 18th century. This book tells the story of the various buildings on the site and by looking at the social history of the area of London around Great Queen Street area explores how freemasonry adapted its buildings to changes in London's history as well as to changes within freemasonry.

As with any book on the history of Freemasons' Hall, this one acknowledges the invaluable work of the late Sir James Stubbs, Past Grand Secretary and Terry Haunch, former Librarian and Curator. Aspects of the 19th century story of the Hall, especially the work of Sir John Soane and John Havers, which have been researched by Douglas Burford, Past Grand Superintendent of Works, have also been drawn on here. Other research is acknowledged in the notes on sources. Both Terry Haunch and Douglas Burford kindly read an early draft and made helpful suggestions.

This book has been written by staff of the Library and Museum of Freemasonry. In 2004 the Library and Museum received a grant from the Heritage Lottery Fund for a project to catalogue and conserve documents relating to the first hundred years of the history of Freemasons' Hall from 1768 to 1868. Over 1,500 documents have been catalogued as a result of this project and are now much more accessible through electronic catalogues available on the internet. Jessica Silver undertook most of this cataloguing work and her knowledge of these documents has helped inform this book. Rebecca Coombes, Katrina Jowett and Amanda David assisted in the development and early stages of the project. Specific contributions have been made by Martin Cherry (the history of the Library and Museum), Emily Greenstreet (the charities) and Alison Royle (on the first Freemasons' Hall medal and the 1869 Steward's jewel). Melrose Eccleston and Peter Aitkenhead researched many of the biographical details. Mark Dennis and Andrew Tucker undertook picture research and much of the photography. Susan Snell suggested a useful approach to the structure of the book. Other Library and Museum staff lead the programme of public tours of the building or take part in open days, which frequently prompts further research in answer to questions raised on those occasions.

Diane Clements
Director
July 2006

A note on measurement and money

All the buildings on the Great Queen Street site were built with imperial measurements. Metric equivalents have been given in the text. All the monetary figures quoted are pre-decimal and decimal equivalents are also given. Monetary values have changed since the 18th century. As a guide the amount of money required today to purchase the goods bought by £1 in 1770 would be £56.50; £1 of goods in 1870 would cost £41.03 today and £1 of goods in 1920 would cost £18.23 today. The estimated cost of the first Hall of £6,500 in 1774 represents a value today of £367, 250. However, other factors are also relevant to a comparison of values, such as the level of wages, and these are not taken into account in these comparative figures.

Introduction

On 24 June 1717 four lodges meeting at the Goose and Gridiron Ale House in St Paul's Churchyard held an Assembly and Feast and formed the Grand Lodge of England, presided over by a Grand Master and his Wardens, thereby establishing the first governing body for freemasonry. The Grand Lodge soon adopted the bureaucratic form that helped to foster the growth of speculative freemasonry with a Grand Secretary and a Book of Constitutions and, by 1723, it was keeping minutes of its meetings. At this time Grand Lodge was an itinerant body holding its regular quarterly meetings in inns and taverns and its Annual Feast in the halls of city livery companies. The manuscript list of lodges entered into the first Minute Book illustrates that initially the jurisdiction of Grand Lodge was limited to lodges meeting in London or within the 'Bills of Mortality', an area within 10 miles of Charing Cross, but within a few years lodges outside London and abroad were acknowledging the authority of Grand Lodge. According to the *List of Regular Lodges* published in 1768, there were nearly 400 lodges of which over 130 were in London. Each lodge had the right to send its Master as representative to attend meetings of Grand Lodge and, although lodges abroad or in more remote parts of the country were unlikely to do so, accommodating all those that did want to attend was becoming more difficult.

The first steps towards building a hall of its own were taken by Grand Lodge on 28 October 1768 when it adopted a plan 'for the most effectual Means for raising a Fund to build a Hall and purchase Jewels, Furniture, &c., for the Grand Lodge'. London was by then the centre of political, social and commercial life in Britain and, as such, it was the obvious choice for the headquarters of freemasonry. Little progress was made with the project until Robert Edward, 9th Lord Petre, became Grand Master in 1772 and actively interested himself in it. A Hall Committee was appointed, first meeting on 12 May 1773 at the Crown and Anchor Tavern on the Strand, a popular meeting place for Masonic lodges (and for the Grand Lodge itself), and began to look for a suitable site. Consideration was given to a number of sites including property 'relative to the Old Play House in Portugal Street, Lincolns Inn Fields', a property on Ormond Street (rejected as too expensive) and some ground and premises situated on the north side of Fleet Street. Ground and premises on Great Queen Street were first brought to the attention of the Committee on 16 March 1774 by Thomas Dight, a carpenter living close by in Great Wild Street. Alexander McKowl was asked to survey the property, which consisted of two houses with a large garden behind. John Croft and Sir Peter Parker, both members of Somerset House Lodge, were also requested to inspect the premises and they reported at a meeting held two days later that in their opinion 'the premises would answer the purposes of ... [the] Society very compleatly [sic]'. The cost of the purchase, building the new Hall and refurbishing the houses was estimated at £6,500. The transaction was completed in April 1774 when the property was purchased from Edward Beaver whose wife had inherited the Great Queen Street property from her previous husband, Philip Carteret Webb, Solicitor to the Treasury. Webb, politician, barrister and antiquary, had been a member of Globe Lodge.

Dight and McKowl were to continue to be involved with the Hall. Dight, a member of Foundation Lodge from 1775, was subsequently employed on carpentry work in the Hall and made a bookcase in 1777 costing £11 5 shillings (£11.25) for one of the Grand Officers, Rowland Berkeley, which is still in use in the present building. Alexander McKowl, Master Bricklayer, also a resident of Great Wild Street, was later contracted for the brickwork for the Hall. He was also a member of Globe Lodge (now No 23), Corinthian Lodge and a Grand Steward in 1775.

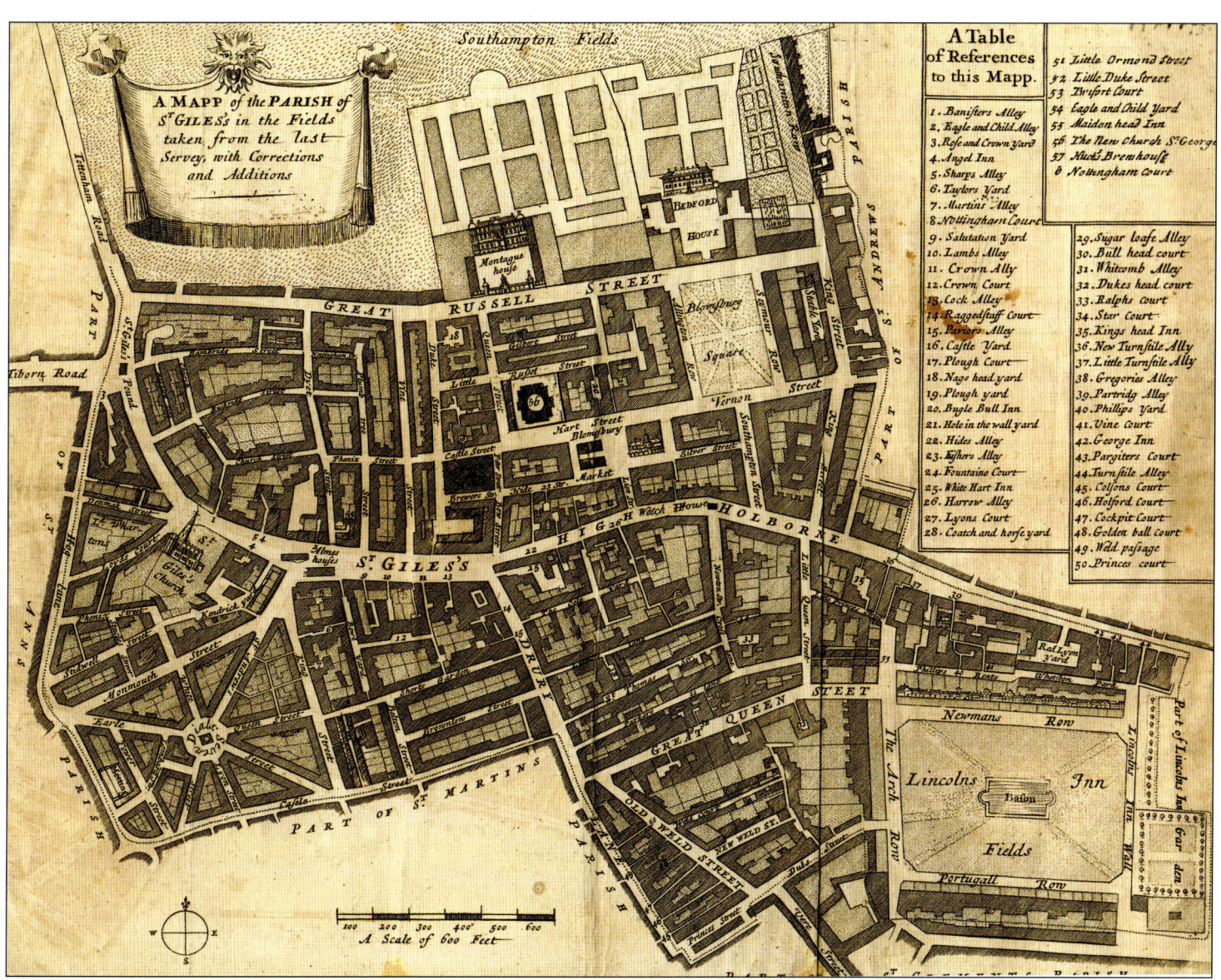

Map of St Giles Parish by John Stow (1633).

Great Queen Street and its Environs in the 18th Century

In 1700 London's population was about 575,000, the same as that of Paris. By 1750 this had grown to 650,000 and had risen still further to just over a million by 1801. Changes in the methods of agricultural and industrial production were making Britain amongst the wealthiest of European nations and prosperity stimulated the growth of a middle class and what has been described as 'the birth of a consumer society'. London was becoming increasingly urbanised. Other developments such as the building of Westminster Bridge (1738-50), only the second Thames crossing after London Bridge in the city, and Blackfriars Bridge (1769) improved communications with areas to the south of the river.

Great Queen Street lay between the cities of London (the commercial capital) and Westminster (the political capital) on the eastern edge of the parish of St Giles in the fields adjacent to Lincoln's Inn Fields. The parish of St Giles had developed as a prosperous village around the chapel of a medieval leper hospital from the early 12th century. The hospital was closed in 1539 but new churches were built on the site of the chapel in 1623 and 1733 (the present church). Until the end of the 16th century the area that was to become Great Queen Street had been largely open country cut across by a track used by James I and his court as a route between Whitehall Palace and the country house of Theobalds in Hertfordshire. Urbanisation began early in the 17th century there, at the southern end of Drury Lane and in Lincoln's Inn Fields. The first houses were built on the north side of what was to become Great Queen Street in the period 1603-12. In 1635 William Newton acquired a licence to build houses and coach houses or stables on the south side of Queen Street (the street being named after Anne of Denmark, the wife of James I). The house that became the first Freemasons' Hall (61 Great Queen Street) was in the middle of the row and was built in 1637. The first occupants of it and other houses in the street (and Drury Lane) were nobility but by the early 18th century they had moved to the more fashionable areas further west and Great Queen Street had become popular with artists. Sir Godfrey Kneller moved there in 1703 where he established his Academy for Painting and Drawing. At his death in 1723 he owned numbers 55, 56, 57 and 58. Other artists who lived there in the 18th century included Thomas Hudson (at 61 from 1747-64), John Opie (at 63 from 1783-91), James Basire at 31 (where his apprentice William Blake also worked from 1773-1778) and Henry Fuseli (at 7 from 1803).

To the east of Newton's development, 67 Great Queen Street was occupied from 1761 to 1784 by the Reverend Thomas Francklin who preached sermons at a chapel built in its grounds. After his death the house and the one adjacent to it were sold for the construction of a new Wesleyan Chapel, which was opened in 1817. Running south from Great Queen Street, Wild Street (Great Wild Street until 1905) existed first as a track. A house built on the east side of the street was purchased in 1651 by Sir Humphrey Weld (the name 'Wild' is a corruption of this). This was demolished in the 1690s and a development of smaller houses and streets (including Wild Court) was built on the site of the house and its garden. Amongst the 18th century residents of Wild Court were the actor Theophilus Cibber.

Around Great Queen Street was one of the better areas of St Giles. In the poorer parts of the parish, especially to the north of the church, the area became known as a centre for drunkenness and crime. Hogarth's satirical painting *Gin Lane* with its view of the characteristic steeple of St George's Church, Bloomsbury, in the background is clearly located in the parish.

To the south-west of Great Queen Street lay the Covent Garden development, designed by Inigo Jones in 1629-37 for the 4th Earl of Bedford as the first of London's squares. Initially a very fashionable address, the growth of a fruit and vegetable market in the centre of the square led the fashionable residents to move west and by the middle of the 18th century the houses on the Piazza had became coffee houses, lodgings and brothels.

The First Freemasons' Hall

The site of 61 Great Queen Street had a frontage of 44ft (13.4m) and a depth of 200ft (60.9m). There was a house at the front divided into two and a small house at the rear, which may have been one of the coach houses of the original scheme.

Thomas Sandby (c1723-98) first attended the Hall Committee on 11 February 1774. He had been working at Windsor for many years and had been in charge of an extensive building campaign at the Great Lodge there since 1757. By 1764 he was steward to Henry Frederick, Duke of Cumberland, and deputy ranger of Windsor Great Park. The Duke had become a freemason in 1767 and was to be Grand Master from 1782-90. Sandby's own lodge membership has never been traced but his links with one of the Craft's Royal patrons as well as his status as a founder member of the Royal Academy and its first Professor of Architecture was sufficient recommendation for his appointment as Grand Architect by Grand Lodge, a rank especially created for him.

Sandby produced several plans for the Hall which were discussed by the Committee. An anonymous plan, presumably by him and recording the agreed design, is included in the third volume of the Hall Committee minutes. Building work commenced and the Hall Committee set about organising the ceremony to mark the laying of the foundation stone. This took place on 1 May 1775 with full Masonic ceremonial, which included a procession and the performance of an ode. An oration was delivered by James Bottomley in which he implored the 'ingenious architect' in the design of the Hall 'to spare no needful cost, to make it strong, to make it rich and beautiful, that in future ages, if no fatal catastrophe befalls it, the wondering beholder may cause to say, sure, something great and good is in this masonry, that its votaries have with such profession, expended treasure, displayed such art, such grandeur and such elegance in adorning this their house'.

The Hall itself had no street frontage. It was built in the garden behind the house on the street with the floor of the Hall raised to the level of the first floor creating a substantial vault or basement below. It was built of brick not stone. It was 78ft (24m) long, 58ft (17.8m) high and 43ft (13.2m) wide. The walls were decorated with pilasters and square fluted columns. Over the entablature at each side of the Hall were semicircular windows, which provided light but were high enough to prevent activities in the Hall being overlooked by adjacent houses. The building of the Hall proceeded quickly and on 2 December 1775 Sandby reported to the Committee that the ceiling of the Hall was 'in a proper condition to receive the ornaments and decorations'. He subsequently produced a design for the plasterwork decoration of the ceiling, which was approved by the Hall Committee and was realised by Richard Cox, the plaisterer. In the centre of this ceiling 'within a large circle, is represented the sun in burnished gold, surrounded by the twelve signs of the zodiac, which are distinguished by their respective symbols. All the other parts are wrought with numerous intersecting circles, including suns, stars etc.' At

The seal of the Grand Lodge, which commissioned the first Freemasons' Hall, shown on a Chinese porcelain bowl.

Admiral Sir Peter Parker.

Thomas Sandby.

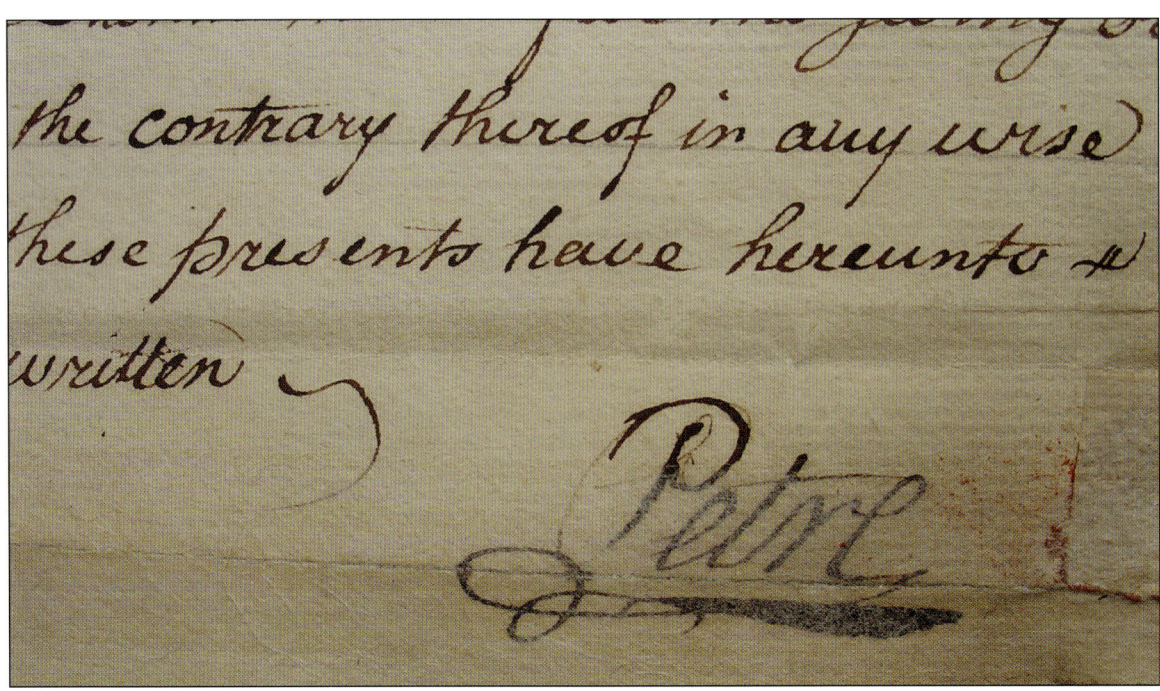

The signature of Lord Petre in the Hall Committee minutes.

the north end of the Hall was an alcove with a gilded keystone and rays emanating from it.

At the same December meeting Sandby reported to the Committee 'that it was customary in building to give a treat to the workmen when the building is covered in — and that the workmen were dissatisfied at the omission of the custom'. Therefore it was agreed to hold a dinner at 2 shillings (10p) per head for all the workmen employed in building the Hall. Members of the Hall Committee dined alongside them 'to encourage the workmen to be diligent in their respective employments'.

The Hall was dedicated on 23 May 1776, attendance was by ticket only and women were admitted during parts of the ceremony. The ceremony included processions around the Hall dedicating it to Masonry, Virtue and Universal Charity and Benevolence. A new ode written especially for the occasion was performed to music by the composer and violinist, John Abraham Fisher, a member of Somerset House Lodge. The music was later the subject of a bitter dispute between Fisher and the Hall Committee concerning who owned the right to have the music printed. The Reverend Dr Dodd, Grand Chaplain, gave an oration. William Dodd (1729-77) was nicknamed the Macaroni parson. After a brief literary career he was ordained at Cambridge University and built a reputation as a preacher. Inclined to live beyond his means, he opened an unsuccessful private school on the basis of his role as tutor to Philip Stanhope, Earl of Chesterfield. The school failed when Stanhope went abroad on the Grand Tour. A year after the Dedication Dodd was arrested for discounting a forged bill of exchange allegedly drawn by the Earl of Chesterfield and tried and hanged at Tyburn despite a popular campaign against his execution.

The Chevalier Ruspini leads a procession of girls from the Royal Cumberland School during a fundraising dinner, showing the interior of Sandby's Hall.

As well as freemasonry, Dodd was involved with a number of charitable and campaigning organisations including the Society for the Relief and Discharge of Persons Imprisoned for Small Debts and the Royal Humane Society.

In June 1780 a week of anti-Catholic rioting erupted in the streets of London focusing on the petition to repeal the Catholic Relief Act of 1778 organised by General George Gordon. Amongst the main targets of the rioters were the Catholic embassy chapels including the Sardinian Chapel in Lincoln's Inn Fields as well as prisons, a distillery in Holborn owned by a Catholic and the bridges across the Thames. It was necessary to protect other buildings and on 1 July 1780, the Hall Committee recorded its thanks to John Hull, the commanding officer of the Royal Volunteers, for 'protecting Freemasons' Hall against the outrages of the mob'.

With the Hall built on the ground behind the two houses, the front house was initially let to John Brooks, a paper-stainer, and part of the back house to Luke Reilly. Grand Lodge retained parts of the back house as committee rooms and offices. Reilly opened a coffee house on his premises, which became the Freemasons' Tavern and Coffee House. He subsequently took over the front house when Brooks surrendered his lease. Although the Hall Committee was concerned that the street frontage should look respectable and there are references to it being whitewashed and later an idea of adding Coade stone decorations, the only public acknowledgement of the use of the site was the erection of a sign showing the Free Masons' Arms with the motto *Vide, Audi, Tace*, the motto subsequently adopted in a slight rearrangement, by the United Grand Lodge for its coat of arms after 1813. The Tavern was demolished and rebuilt in 1788-9 (designed by Sandby assisted by William Tyler, sculptor and architect of the Ordnance office in Westminster) and became four storeys high with a stone facing up to the second floor. In 1791 the tenants of the Tavern successfully submitted plans for building a new kitchen in the garden of the adjoining house to the east (62 Great Queen Street), the lease of which had just been acquired by Grand Lodge, to replace the existing inadequate kitchen facilities. It was the beginning of a gradual expansion of the original site that was not to be completed until the 20th century.

One of the First Violin parts of the music written by John Abraham Fisher in 1776 for the Dedication ceremony.

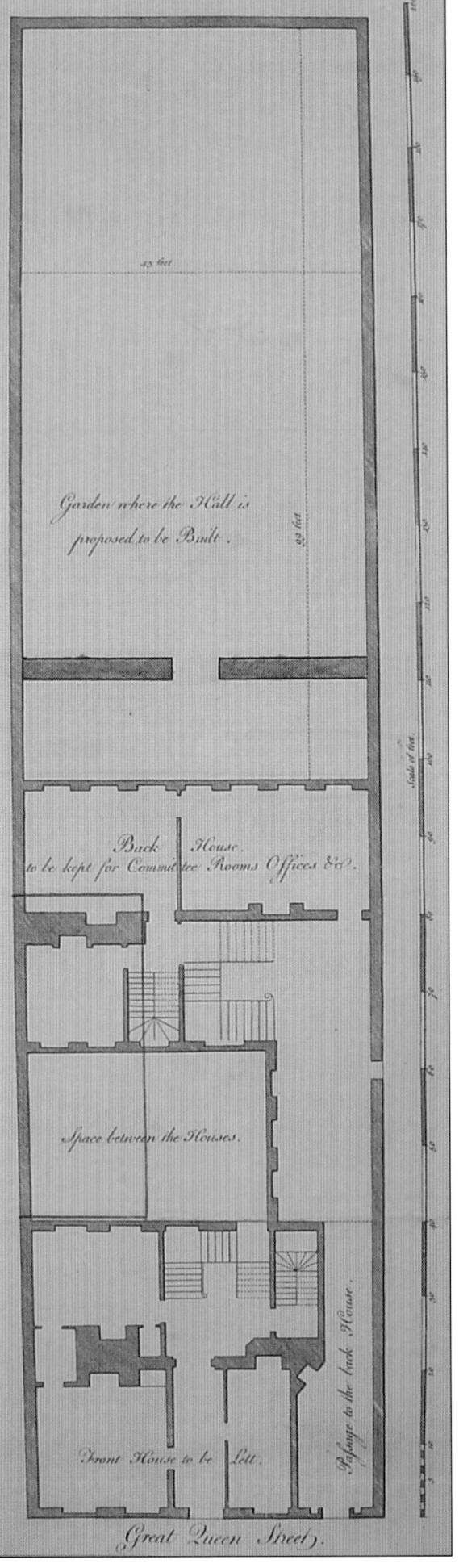

Plan of the site showing the Hall to be built in the garden behind the houses fronting the street.

The frontage of the Wesleyan Chapel in the early nineteenth century.

Paying for the Hall

The funds of Grand Lodge were primarily raised to support 'any true brother fallen into poverty or decay'. A scheme for financing the building of a Hall and providing for its furniture had first been put forward with the original 1768 proposal and included the introduction of a scale of annual contributions by Grand Officers and set charges for services performed by Grand Lodge such as registering new members. This led to the introduction of a series of registers, organised by lodge, recording individual members, based on annual returns submitted by lodges with the appropriate fees. By 1774 when an Extraordinary Grand Lodge was convened at the London Tavern to ascertain what money could be raised to purchase the Great Queen Street site, these fees had contributed £760 to a Building Fund.

Other funds were raised from donations (£660 was donated at the March 1774 Extraordinary Grand Lodge) or loans but one of the principal fundraising schemes was a tontine, a method often employed at the time to finance building projects. The 1775 Freemasons' Tontine offered one hundred shares costing £50 each, thus raising £5,000. For each share they bought, subscribers had to nominate themselves or another individual of any age who was known as the 'nominee'. The subscribers to the scheme did not receive back their £50 subscription (the principal element of the loan) but each nominee received a one hundredth share of an annual £250 dividend payment. The total dividend amount remained the same, but the payment for each individual share increased as the number of living nominees became fewer; the last surviving nominee was therefore entitled to the entire £250 dividend. The last surviving member of the Freemasons' Tontine was Ann Ellis who had been just two years old when her father, Admiral Sir Peter Parker, had nominated her. Her death in 1862 at the age of 89 meant that Grand Lodge had paid out a total of £21,750 in dividend payments throughout the time the scheme was in operation.

The total cost of the site and the building work was nearly £15,000 instead of the £6,500 originally estimated. Despite extended delays in paying the tradesmen involved — some were still owed money as late as 1785 — further funds were required. At a meeting on 29 May 1779 the Committee 'took into consideration . . . proposals for raising money to pay off the Hall Debt' and agreed 'that a subscription be entered into of a sum not less than £25 each, and the money raised thereby to be lent to the Society without interest . . . [and] that as a mark of distinction for the services rendered to the Society by this subscription . . . each subscriber shall be complimented with a medal of such form and value as the Grand Lodge shall think proper with a motto suitable to the occasion and that the . . . subscribers shall be entered in the books of the Grand Lodge as an honourable testimonial of their services'. It was also agreed that if a lodge subscribed to the scheme the lodge would be presented with the medal. In February 1780 the Committee met to consider the designs put

Right:
The 1780 Hall Medal.

Far right:
The 1780 Hall Medal (reverse). This medal belonged to the Chevalier Ruspini.

THE ORIGINAL SUBSCRIBERS TO THE FREE-MASONS TONTINE:

WITH THE

Number of Lives for which each have subscribed.

[1775.]

	Lives.		Lives.
THE Right Hon. and Most Worshipful Lord PETRE	4	Joshua Lara, Esq;	1
His Royal Highness the Duke of Cumberland	2	George Harrison, Esq;	1
His Grace the Duke of Beaufort	5	Mr. John Cotterell	1
Rowland Holt, Esq;	2	Mr. Thomas Fothergill	1
Thomas Parker, Esq;	2	Mr. James Galloway	2
John Croft, Esq;	2	Mr. Thomas Pownall	4
Sir Peter Parker	2	Mr. John Lodge	1
William Atkinson, Esq;	1	Mr. Edward Parish	1
William Hodgson, Esq;	2	Mr. John Yeomans *Theophilus*	1
Charles Taylor, Esq;	1	Mr. Thomas Thompson Tutt	2
Mr. Henry Jaffray	1	James Harrison, Esq;	1
Henry Dagge, Esq;	1	Mr. Robert Groome	1
John Deaken, Esq;	1	Mr. Benjamin Johnson	1
Thomas Dunckerley, Esq;	2	Mr. Robert Hull	1
John Allen, Esq;	2	Mr. Charles Iliffe	1
Thomas Minshall, Esq;	1	Bartholomew Ruspini, Esq;	1
Thomas Fowke, Esq;	1	John Wilkinson, Esq;	1
Rowland Berkeley, G. T.	2	Mr. James Mist	2
James Heseltine, G. S.	2	Raphael Franco, Esq;	2
Mr. John Derwas	2	Dr. Sequiera	3
Benjamin Lyons, Esq;	2	Mr. Samuel Wright	1
Mr. Thomas Settree	1	Charles Hanbury, Esq;	1
Mr. William Settree	1	Richard Rous, Esq;	1
Mr. William Cole	9	Thomas B. Calley, Esq;	1
Mr. James White	1	Lewis Poignand, Esq;	1
Mr. Stephen Clarke	1	Thomas Sandby, Esq;	1
Mr. William White	1	James Bottomley, Esq;	1
Richard Douglas, Esq;	2	Edward Clough, Esq;	1
Isaac Pereyra, Esq;	7		100

Subscription list for the Freemasons' Tontine.

Frontispiece of the 1784 Book of Constitutions.

forward for the medal and the design by Edward Parker, a professional seal engraver, was chosen in a secret ballot. Lewis Pingo, the chief engraver to the Royal Mint who had earlier produced medals for the Royal Humane Society, struck the dies for the medal. The medal was silver gilt and neo-Classical in design. On the obverse, a winged and draped female figure stood languidly next to a Doric column. In her right hand she held a style with which she inscribed on the column 'IN / HONOUR / OF THE / SUBSCRI [bers]'. In her left hand she held a trumpet and a scroll bearing the façade of a Classical building. To the left of the column was a building under construction surrounded by scaffolding. The scene is a covered with the sun's rays. Below the scene the jewel bore the date MDCCLXXX (1780). On the reverse of the medal was the presentation inscription. The text, in relief, read 'GRAND LODGE OF FREE MASONS IN ENGLAND / TO / [a brother] / IN GRATEFUL / TESTIMONY / OF A LIBERAL / SUBSCRIPTION / TOWARDS / COMPLEATING / THEIR HALL'. Subscriptions to the scheme began slowly. At the beginning of 1783 only 46 brethren and 9 lodges had subscribed. On 8 January 1783, at a special meeting of Grand Lodge it was decided that, in addition to receipt of the Hall medal, subscribers would receive a number of supplementary benefits. The most notable of these was permission to attend meetings of Grand Lodge, regardless of their Masonic rank. Lodges who subscribed to the scheme were permitted to send a fourth representative to Grand Lodge meetings, in addition to the Master and his Wardens. These privileges were to be relinquished once the loan had been repaid. However, after the Union of the two rival Grand Lodges in 1813, the new Book of Constitutions made no mention of the privileges, forcing those Brethren and Lodges that had not yet been repaid to relinquish them. The final total of subscribers was reached in 1786 — 82 brethren and 26 lodges, giving a total of £2,600. Of the 108 subscribers, 40 converted their loans to donations and 21 had their loans repaid in part or in full. For the remaining there are no records.

As another way of helping to finance the cost of the Hall, Grand Lodge agreed to publish a new edition of the Book of Constitutions which was to include 'an elegant Frontispiece' showing the interior of the Hall no doubt to encourage members of lodges that their money had been put to good use and also to be a marketing tool for future potential hirers. The frontispiece accompanying this 1784 Book of Constitutions was drawn by Giovanni Battista Cipriani with the assistance of Sandby and engraved by Francesco Bartolozzi. Both Cipriani and Bartolozzi were members of the Lodge of the Nine Muses. Cipriani's image was dominated by emblematical characters and showed the Hall as an almost empty space with the furniture used for a Grand Lodge meeting being portable and brought in to the Hall for such meetings.

It was at a meeting held on 19 September 1775, before the Hall was even completed, that the minutes record for the first time an application by a non-Masonic group requesting the use of the premises owned by the Society. The minutes record that it was agreed to 'receive a company who propose to have a Dancing Company in the Committee Room'. Reilly, the tenant of the Freemasons' Tavern, assured the committee that he 'would make good any damage that might arise to the Society's rooms'. A year later a letter from Sir Charles Whitworth, politician and writer, was read 'offering twenty guineas for the use of the Hall for a select musical meeting once a week for ten weeks'. This arrangement was rejected by the Committee as the Hall was 'not yet finished, nor in a proper state for the reception of company' but a subsequent proposal made in November was accepted.

Francesco Bartolozzi, engraver of the frontispiece of the 1784 Book of Constitutions, which was drawn by his friend Giovanni Cipriani. This engraving is by his pupil Giovanni Vendramini.

In January 1777 more formal regulations concerning the hiring of the Hall were put in place. It was resolved by the Committee that the Hall should not 'be let for the purpose of any dancing masters ball; nor for any concert or ball for a less sum than ten guineas a night. That whoever shall take the Hall shall at the time of the agreement give satisfactory security to the Committee to repair any injury that may be sustained, during the time the Hall is let to them'. By April, John Allen, a member of the Committee

The rules drawn up for users of the Hall.

21ſt Day of *November*, 1779.

TERMS AND REGULATIONS

FOR THE

ASSEMBLIES

INTENDED TO BE HELD AT

FREEMASONS' HALL, Great *Queen-Street*, *Lincoln's-Inn-Fields*,

The enſuing WINTER,

Under the Direction of the Gentlemen who conducted thoſe of the preceding Winters.

I. THAT the Number of Aſſemblies ſhall be Four, *viz.* on the ſecond *Thurſday* in the Months of *January*, *February*, *March*, and *April*, provided the Number of Subſcribers ſhall amount to Sixty, otherwiſe the Subſcription Money to be returned.

II. THAT the Terms of the Subſcription be Three Guineas, for which the Subſcriber ſhall be entitled to one Gentleman's and two Ladies Tickets each Aſſembly.

III. THAT all Applications for Subſcriptions ſhall be made to the Directors, who will admit Subſcribers, by Ballot, at their Meetings in *Great Queen-Street*, on the *Thurſday* Evening preceding each Aſſembly.

IV. THAT Tickets ſhall be ſent to every Subſcriber, previous to each Aſſembly; and no Ticket will be received for Admiſſion on any other Night, than that for which it is particularly deſigned.

V. THAT a Subſcriber may be at Liberty to introduce a Non-Subſcriber, on applying to the Treaſurer for an extra Ticket for that Purpoſe, paying for the ſame, as follows: For a Gentleman's Half a Guinea, a Lady's Five Shillings; and writing the Name and Place of Abode of

and Provincial Grand Master for Lancashire, was instructed to draw up an agreement to be signed by individuals wishing to use the Hall. These printed agreements were to be bound into a book (which no longer survives). Reductions from the standard charge of 10 guineas (£10.50) per night were often agreed in cases of hardship. The Hall was not one of the most fashionable venues in London (being some distance from the West End) but it could hold 800 people so was larger than most and particularly suitable for musical performances which needed a choir. The administration of bookings was handled by the landlord of the Tavern making reference to members of the Hall Committee. This practice continued until the building of the second Hall in the 1860s. It tended to lead to some confusion particularly in public notices between whether an event was held in the Hall or the Tavern.

The Academy of Ancient Music had been set up as a private club in the 1720s to perform music of earlier centuries including motets and madrigals. It met in inns and taverns but in 1784 it began a series of public concerts held in the Hall. The musical directors during this period, Benjamin Cooke and Samuel Arnold, were both freemasons. It was in response to a request from this organisation that Grand Lodge installed an organ in the Hall at a cost of 200 guineas (£210). The Hall was also used for events involving readings and music, fashionable in the 1780s and 1790s.

Much of London's (and England's) medical and educational provision was at this time financed by philanthropy. A common fundraising method was a formal dinner and many organisations held dinners in the Hall including the Lloyds Patriotic Fund (which was formed in 1803 to provide financial assistance to the wounded and the families of those killed during the Napoleonic Wars), the Middlesex Hospital (based in Soho), the Benevolent Society for the Delivering of Poor Married Women and the Finsbury Dispensary. The Royal Humane Society, founded in 1774 to advocate saving people from death by resuscitation (then an unproven and somewhat controversial technique), had a long association with the Hall. At its fundraising dinners winners of its medals were paraded around the Hall to applause from the audience. One of the Society's earliest supporters had been the Reverend Dodd who had given the oration at the opening of the Hall. The Secretary to the Society from 1813 to 1820 was Thomas Pettigrew, a freemason and sometime Surgeon and Librarian to the Grand Master, the Duke of Sussex. Masonic charities held similar events. Concerts were held for the benefit of the Royal Cumberland Freemasons' School for the daughters of deceased and indigent freemasons beginning in the year of its foundation in 1788. The girls were paraded round the hall to sing during the concert intervals. One of the most well known of all depictions of the Hall is on one such occasion. Some of Charles Dickens' earliest journalism, first published in the *Evening Chronicle* on 7 April 1835 and subsequently reprinted in his *Sketches by Boz*, describes his attendance at a public dinner in the 1830s for the 'Indigent Orphans Benevolent Institution' at 'the Freemasons'. The meal was served at one of three long tables using knives and forks which 'look as if they had done duty at every public dinner in London since the accession

A theatrical performance in the Hall during the Victorian period.

THEATRICAL FUND DINNER HELD AT FREE-MASONS TAVERN.
PROTEUS (as Treasurer) addressing the Royal Chairman respecting the flourishing state of the Funds —

A Theatrical Fund Dinner held at the Freemasons' Tavern, showing the Duke of Sussex in the Grand Master's throne.

of George I', the music could barely be heard and the speeches and toasts were interminable.

The Hall provided a meeting place for local organisations including the local parish and the Covent Garden Theatrical Fund and the Drury Lane Theatrical Fund (which both supported retired stage performers) and 'National' societies such as the Society of Ancient Britons (for the Welsh), the Highland Society and the Benevolent Society of St Patrick.

The rise of the evangelical movement in the early 19th century fostered a number of campaigning societies which needed a meeting place. In 1831 Exeter Hall in the Strand was opened for their use but Sandby's Hall was often also used. The Church Missionary Society, the British and Foreign Bible Society and the Continental Association (which supported Protestant teaching in Roman Catholic countries) all held meetings there. The Evangelical Alliance was founded in a series of meetings at the Hall in 1846. In December 1856 the London Missionary Society gave a public reception at the Hall to mark David Livingstone's return from Africa. Many of these societies were closely involved with the anti-slavery movement and the Anti-Slavery Society was established at a meeting at the Hall in 1807. Other religious groups were excluded from Exeter Hall with its strong Nonconformist links. A 'Great Meeting of the Catholics of London' addressed by Daniel O'Connell was held at Freemasons' Hall on 15 July 1839 in support of Catholic Emancipation.

By the early 19th century the extensive use of the Hall for non-Masonic events led to it being included in 'The Illustrations of the Public Buildings of London', published by John Britton and Auguste Charles Pugin in 1825 in which it was described as an 'elegant and finely proportioned room, and both in architectural character and decoration is strictly appropriate to the purpose for which it was designed'.

A meeting of the Royal Humane Society.

Sandby's Hall as shown in *Illustrations of the Public Buildings of London*.

The Impact of the Union

In 1813 the Premier Grand Lodge and its rival, the Antients, formed in 1751-3, finally agreed Articles of Union. The Antients had never had a Hall of their own. It was acknowledged in the Articles of Union agreed between the two Grand Lodges that 'the Freemasons' Hall shall be the place in which the United Grand Lodge shall be held' but it was clear that the existing accommodation in Great Queen Street would not be large enough for meetings of the new entity nor to cope with administering the business of over 1,500 lodges worldwide. In 1815 Grand Lodge acquired (with the assistance of John Jackson Cuff, the proprietor of the Freemasons' Tavern) use of the freeholds of the two houses to the east of the existing building, 62 and 63 Great Queen Street. Sir John Soane, Professor of Architecture at the Royal Academy, who had been initiated as a freemason in November 1813 and in the following month appointed to the new office of Grand Superintendant of the Works (sic) by the Duke of Sussex as Grand Master, contributed £500 to assist the purchase. He had surveyed the properties for Grand Lodge as early as 1812. Soane designed new buildings in the yards behind these two houses. Building began in 1828 and took three years to complete. Soane's Hall came to be known first as the New Hall and, from 1837, as the Temple and was only used for Masonic ceremonies. It was not intended to replace Sandby's Hall, which continued to admit the public. The Temple was designed in such a way that the sequence of rooms, their décor and lighting reflected the nature of Masonic ritual. A modern description of Soane's Temple by David Watkin describes it as consisting of 'two long sides featuring end bays containing chimneypieces, with windows oddly placed over them; the centres of the long sides were occupied by tripartite compositions, rather like triumphal arches, in which pedimented false door cases flanked arched and coffered recesses containing on the west side an organ and on the east side a ceremonial throne. The shorter north and south sides each received a similar tripartite treatment, with a throne in the centre of the former, and the main entrance in the centre of the latter. Additional light filtered through four segmental . . . windows, one high up in the centre of each wall and more significantly, from the tall, glazed lantern which surmounted the central hanging canopy.'

Unfortunately for Soane, his Temple was never greatly admired by his fellow Masons. After his death in 1837 the September issue of the 1838 *Freemasons' Quarterly* stated 'The 'New Temple,' Freemasons' Hall, was erected a few years since, from the design, and under the direction of our late Grand Superintendent of Works, and was by him considered to be among the first, if not the very best, of his works. On entering it, every person conversant with his peculiar style of architecture, would at once trace the fanciful genius of Sir John Soane — but we candidly confess we do not like to see 'Defiance hurled at Rome and Greece,' and therefore are not very great admirers of the Soanean style.' The writer considered Soane's Hall to be 'overloaded with ornament, and cut up into too many minor parts, each perfect in itself, but wanting in the perfection of dignity as a whole'.

In 1838, only a year after Soane's death, plans were put forward for extensions and alterations to the Temple. When the freeholds of 62 and 63 Great Queen Street were finally purchased by Grand Lodge in the same year for £8,000, extensions to the premises were made possible. These additions and modifications were designed by Philip Hardwick, Soane's successor to the Masonic office of Grand Superintendent of Works, as the rank became more generally known, who added an apse at one end of Soane's

Sir John Soane. An engraving by John Thomson after the portrait by Sir Thomas Lawrence.

The Duke of Sussex, Grand Master of the United Grand Lodge of England 1813-1843. A copy of a portrait in Highland dress by Sir William Beechey.

Illuminated address presented to Soane by the Grand Lodge in 1821 for 'the judicious and able manner in which the several repairs and improvements have been made'.

Temple and provided a room for a Library. Hardwick (1792-1870), a founder member of the Institute of British Architects, was noted for his work in the classical style for a number of institutions including Goldsmiths' Hall (1829-35), the arch at Euston Station (demolished 1961-2) and a new hall, council room and library for Lincoln's Inn which used wrought and cast iron extensively in the construction of its roof. He was initiated in the Prince of Wales's Lodge (now No 259) in May 1831 and was Grand Superintendent of Works 1837-55.

Furnishing the Hall

In 1790 George, Prince of Wales, was elected Grand Master and, conscious of the new status this gave, in February 1791, Grand Lodge resolved that chairs and candlesticks for the use of Grand Lodge should be provided. The Hall Committee was to receive designs and estimates for candlesticks which should be 'of brass lacquered, made large and elegantly finished'. They were made by William Bent. Robert Kennett's basic chair designs, in the French style admired by the Prince of Wales, were approved, as was his proposal to cover the chairs with garter blue velvet. The chairs were, however, a rare case when the Committee gave specific design instructions: 'Directions were also given to Mr Kennett to make the columns or Pillars of the Chairs strictly conformable to the order and usage of the society viz. the Grand Master's to be of the Doric Order, the Senior Warden the Ionic Order and the Junior Warden's the Corinthian Order'.

Robert Kennett was an established cabinet-maker and upholsterer with a workshop in New Bond Street. He had already supplied chairs for Badminton House for the 5th Duchess of Beaufort. Her husband had been Grand Master from 1767 to 1771. Chairs commissioned for use by Masonic lodges and decorated with the orders of architecture were not a new idea. Earlier examples can be seen in the collection of the Library and Museum in London such as those owned by Britannic Lodge No 33 and dated to 1760-80. But what exactly was the 'usage of the society' had not been finalised at this point. The chairs belonging to Britannic Lodge had Corinthian pillars on the Master's chair and Ionic on the Warden's Chair. Although there are earlier examples, William Preston (1742-1818), at one time a member of the Hall Committee, was one of the principal writers responsible for the wider dissemination of knowledge of the Five Orders of Architecture into Masonic thought, originally in the Second Lecture of his 1781 edition of Illustrations of Masonry and then in the large number of subsequent editions. Masonic usage linked the orders of architecture with particular attributes and lodge officers. The idea of pillars or columns, usually three in number, came to symbolise a number of concepts. They were regarded as the emblematic supports of a mason's lodge called Wisdom, Strength and Beauty. In turn the attributes were applied to lodge officers with the Master being Wisdom, the Senior Warden, Strength and the Junior Warden, Beauty. The link between specific orders and these attributes was developing in the late 18th century. By the 1820s this had been fixed so that the Master was represented by the Ionic Order, the Senior Warden by the Doric Order and the Junior Warden represented by the Corinthian order, an alternative arrangement to that actually used by Kennett on the instructions of the Committee as can still be seen on the chairs.

The chairs were not, however, the first decorations in the Hall. Whether he had intended it or not, Sandby's Hall provided wall spaces for full-length portraits. In June 1785 the artist Matthew William Peters wrote to the Grand Secretary offering to present his portrait of Lord Petre 'for the adornment of [the] Hall'. Shortly

The Grand Master's throne designed by Robert Kennett showing the ducal coronet for the Duke of Connaught, replacing the original Prince of Wales' feathers.

Photograph of Sandby's Hall showing how the Wardens' chairs were covered and stored at one end of the Hall when not in use.

The frontispiece of the 1815 Constitutions of the new United Grand Lodge shows the Ark of the Masonic Covenant by the left-hand side of the figure. Engraved by Brother Silvester.

thereafter he presented a portrait of George, 4th Duke of Manchester, and, in due course, portraits of Henry Frederick, Duke of Cumberland, and the Prince of Wales. On the recommendation of the Duke of Manchester he was appointed Grand Portrait Painter in 1785, the only person to have held such a title. Peters (1742-1814) had trained as an artist in London with Thomas Hudson and also studied in Italy. He became a member of Somerset House Lodge in 1769. By the time he approached Grand Lodge, Peters had embarked on another career having been ordained as a priest in 1782. He was later Chaplain to the Prince of Wales. He was appointed Provincial Grand Master of Lincolnshire in 1792. Portraits of Edward, Duke of Kent, and Augustus Frederick, Duke of Sussex, for the Hall were later painted by Sir William Beechey. An organ, the work of Samuel Green, was installed at the south end in 1787 to support the concerts and musical events by non-Masonic users of the Hall such as the Academy of Ancient Music. Matthew William Peters painted an oval half-length portrait of George III to decorate this. After the Union in 1813 portraits of some of the Grand Masters of the Antients Grand Lodge were added. Most of these portraits were destroyed in the fire at the Hall in 1883 (see below).

In anticipation of the Union between the two Grand Lodges, in August 1813 Sir John Soane was asked by the Duke of Sussex to design and construct an Ark of the Masonic Covenant to house the document setting out the Articles of Union. Soane's Ark of the Masonic Covenant was not based on the biblical description of the original Ark of the Covenant in the Bible although it was this form which had previously featured on the arms of the Antients Grand Lodge and was to feature on the new arms of the United Grand Lodge.

Soane's Ark was lost in a fire at Freemasons' Hall in May 1883 but details of it survive in a detailed press report given immediately after the fire, in designs in the Soane archives and in a number of images. It was made of mahogany, triangular in plan and in the form of a pedestal cabinet, and was not meant to be transportable like the biblical Ark. Its entablature was supported at the corners by the three classical orders of architecture and was surmounted by a triangular based dome. The Ark measured in height about 3ft 6in (1.1m) to the top of the entablature and about 4ft 3in (1.3m) to the top of the dome. The sides of the equilateral triangular base measured about 3ft 4in (1m) and the columns at the corners were set about 2ft (0.6m) apart.

Matthew William Peters, Grand Portrait Painter. An engraving by William Satchwell Leney after a self portrait.

Portrait of George III by Peters used to decorate the front of the organ in the Hall.

Edward Hodges Baily.

In the early years of the 19th century other items of furniture were obtained for the Hall. In June 1820 the Grand Master, the Duke of Sussex, presented to the Hall 'an elegantly carved and gilt chair, the back and seat covered with rich purple velvet to be used as the Chair of the Deputy Grand Master and also four smaller chairs to correspond as seats for the Past Grand Masters or other Brethren of High Rank and Distinction'. Then in March 1834 two further chairs are recorded for use by the Grand Secretaries (there being two at this time), 'two large richly carved elbow chairs, gilt, with purple velvet backs and seats, and a large table with an Embroiderd Cover'. In 1821 the minutes of Grand Lodge refer to the payment of £70 to Sir George Nayler for banners. Nayler was Clarenceux King of Arms at the College of Arms and a noted expert on heraldry. He was a member of the Lodge of Antiquity (now No 2) and Grand Director of Ceremonies. Unfortunately there are no surviving records of these banners or how they

Memorandum of Agreement

made and entered into this Third day of April One thousand eight hundred and forty four **Between** The Right Honorable Thomas Earl of Zetland, Alexander Dobie of Lancaster Place Strand Gentleman and Philip Hardwick of Russell Square Architect three of the Committee appointed by the Grand Lodge of England to carry into execution the Vote of the Grand Lodge that a Statue be Erected to the Memory of the late Most Illustrious Grand Master His Royal Highness Prince Augustus Frederick Duke of Sussex K.G. &c &c &c of the one part and Edward Hodges Baily Esquire R.A. and F.R.S of the other part

Whereas it has been proposed by the said Thomas Earl of Zetland Alexander Dobie and Philip Hardwick to have executed a Marble Statue to perpetuate the memory of His late Royal Highness The Most Illustrious Grand Master of Masons agreeably to the Vote of the Grand Lodge of the Seventh day of June last and it has been agreed by the said Thomas Earl of Zetland Alexander Dobie and Philip Hardwick on behalf of the Grand Lodge and the said Edward Hodges Baily as follows, that is to say,—

First — **That** the said Edward Hodges Baily shall be and is hereby appointed the Sculptor for carrying the above recited object into effect to the extent and in the manner hereinafter mentioned.—

Second — **That** the Statue so to be executed by the said Edward Hodges Baily shall be made of the best White Carrara Marble and be such as is usually employed and used by Sculptors in England in similar Works of Art and shall be of one piece and measure not less than seven feet from the top of the head to the sole of the feet.—

Third — **That** the said Statue shall stand on a Pedestal of Rochabby Stone six feet six inches high and about three feet six inches wide and have an appropriate Inscription and Emblems cut thereon. The front Pannel for the said Inscription and the said Emblems to be of the best White Carrara Marble.—

Fourth — **That** the said Statue and Pedestal shall be finished delivered and

The agreement between Grand Lodge and Edward Hodges Baily.

were displayed. They may have been the coats of arms of the Grand Masters that were displayed above their portraits. Grand Lodge also commissioned portrait busts of its Royal Grand Masters. Busts of George IV and the Duke of Sussex (both by Sir Francis Chantrey), William IV and Edward, Duke of Kent, (both by John Francis) and of Frederick, Duke of York, (by Edward Hodges Baily after Nollekens) were acquired in this way.

The Duke of Sussex, who had become Grand Master at the Union, died on 21 April 1843, after dominating English freemasonry for over 30 years. At the next meeting of Grand Lodge in June 1843, it was decided that Grand Lodge would set up a fund with an initial donation of £1,000 which would be used to erect what was described as 'a suitable Masonic Testimonial' to the Duke. A committee including the Earl of Zetland, the Pro Grand Master at that time, the Grand Treasurer, the Grand Superintendent of Works and the Grand Secretary was established. This committee was later supplemented by others including Benjamin Bond Cabbell, the Treasurer of the Girls' School, and the Duke's former opponent, Robert Crucefix. It decided that a statue in Freemasons' Hall would be the best tribute and a budget of £1,800 was set.

The Committee chose to commission one of the leading sculptors of the time — Edward Hodges Baily. Baily had been a pupil at the Royal Academy of Art and had built up a reputation as a designer of silver for the leading goldsmiths of the time, Rundell, Bridge & Rundell and Paul Storr. He had sculpted stone pieces for Buckingham House (later Palace) and marble for a number of noble patrons. He had won second prize in the Nelson memorial competition in 1839 and was allocated the figure of Nelson which was raised to the top of its column in Trafalgar Square in November 1843.

The first payment of £600 was made to Baily in March 1844. The actual agreement with him is dated 3 April 1844. It specified that the statue was to be made of one piece of the best white Carrara marble and to measure at least 7ft (2.15m) high. Its pedestal was to be 6ft 6in (2m) high and 3ft 6in (1.1m) wide. Baily is recorded as joining Jerusalem Lodge No 97 in London on 10 April 1844. (The entry in the membership register shows him joining from Lodge No 79, but no earlier lodge membership or initiation has been traced.) He served as Master of the lodge in 1847 when he was also a Grand Steward. He also joined the Prince of Wales's Lodge No 259 in April 1845 but all his Masonic memberships had lapsed by 1853.

By December 1844 it was reported that Baily had completed his model of the statue and the final work was complete by early 1846 (the agreement had specified 3 April) as on 29 April, the Earl of Zetland unveiled the marble statue placed in the recess at the eastern end of the Hall. It was described as 'equally distinguished for the truthfulness of the portraiture and its beauty as a work of art'.

The statue suffered superficial damage in the fire of 1883 but was cleaned and reinstated on its pedestal in the refurbished Hall.

The plans for the construction of the Masonic Peace Memorial Building after the 1914-1918 War had envisaged the retention of Sandby's Temple and no thought had been given as to any need to accommodate the statue elsewhere. When the decision was taken to demolish this Hall (see below), the new Grand Temple had already been completed and a new location had to be found. The statue was very heavy and had to be retained at ground floor level. It was finally placed in a corridor near the Board Room but its pedestal was removed.

The statue of the Duke of Sussex at the eastern end of Sandby's Hall.

Baily's statue of the Duke of Sussex waiting for its home in the Masonic Peace Memorial Building.

Engraving of the installation of the Prince of Wales as Grand Master in 1875, showing both the chair and Soane's Ark of the Masonic Covenant.

Sandby's Hall after the fire of 1883.

The Sussex statue shown in the current building.

Great Queen Street and its Environs in the 19th Century

In 1862, George Routledge, a member of Royal Somerset House and Inverness Lodge (now No 4) published his *Popular Guide to London and the Suburbs* in which London was described as 'the political, moral, physical, intellectual, artistic, literary, commercial and social centre of the world'. London's population in 1851 was 2.3 million people and over 4.5 million by 1901.

It was the era of improvements coinciding with a desire to improve social conditions. In London this meant improvements in communications as the creation of major thoroughfares was often linked with plans to eliminate overcrowded slum areas that were the focus for disease. Most of the slums or 'rookeries' of St Giles were removed to allow for the creation of a new road, New Oxford Street, in 1841-7 to provide a more direct link between High Holborn and Oxford Street. Endell Street providing a north-south link to Covent Garden was built at the same time. The other notorious slum area around Seven Dials was cleared gradually from the 1840s to the 1880s and commercial and industrial buildings such as breweries replaced the slums. Two other road schemes, the creation of Shaftesbury Avenue in 1877-86 and Charing Cross Road laid out in 1887, also improved the communications of the area.

Communications were also improved by new types of transport including the horse drawn omnibus which first ran on a route from Paddington to Bank via Islington in 1829 and later throughout London. This was pioneered by George Shillibeer (1797-1866) who trained as a coachbuilder in Long Acre (the centre of the trade in London). Railways and competition soon undermined the financial success of his business and he later patented a new type of funeral carriage and set up in business as an undertaker. Shillibeer was initiated in Etonian Lodge (now No 209), Windsor in 1827 and joined Globe Lodge (now No 23) in 1829. The building of another new bridge — Waterloo Bridge (1817) — linked the Strand to the Surrey side of the river whilst links between the City and Westminster, the expanding suburbs and the rest of the country were increased with the development of the railway system and their termini, including Charing Cross station (1863-5) at the western end of the Strand, and the first underground railways.

The need to improve the sewerage system, which could only be done on a co-ordinated basis, prompted the formation of the Metropolitan Board of Works in 1855. London eventually acquired a single administrative body, the London County Council, in 1888. Great Queen Street became part of the Borough of Holborn.

Individuals also undertook philanthropy. William Williams had established one of the first 'Ragged Schools' in the St Giles Rookery in 1843. Having attracted the interest of Lord Shaftesbury, the St Giles and St George's Refuge for Homeless and Destitute Boys, precursor of the Shaftesbury Homes, was established towards the eastern end of the north side of Great Queen Street around the middle of the century. The Society for the Improvement of the Labouring Classes took over the ownership of a large number of poorer quality properties in Wild Court in 1854 for renovation. The Society also built model houses in Little Wild Street to the south of Wild Court. Peabody Buildings on the west side of Wild Street, built in 1880, was another development of model housing originally for poorer families financed by the American-born banker George Peabody. These initiatives did not necessarily solve the problem of poor living conditions as in Charles Booth's *Inquiry into the Life and Labour of the People in London* (1886-1903) the south side of Great Queen Street adjacent to Freemasons' Hall was shown as middle class and well to do but Great Wild Street was shown as an area of the very poor, only undertaking casual work and in chronic want as were many of the people living in the housing to the south of the Hall off Drury Lane. Residents of parts of Parker Street to the north of the Hall were in the lowest class, vicious and semi-criminal. Other social developments were also reflected in the occupation of Great Queen Street properties. Number 36 on the north side was the headquarters of the Women's Protective & Provident League, a group of trades unions for women founded in 1874 by Emma Paterson.

The growth of London's population and its need for fruit and vegetables encouraged the continued growth of the market in Covent Garden and the building of the Market House (1828-30), the Flower Market (1871-87) and the Jubilee Hall (1904) as permanent buildings on the site. The Market provided employment for many local residents but there were a wide variety of other local industries. The staple trades of Great Queen Street tended to be bookselling, bookbinding and publishing (including the business of Richard Spencer at 26 Great Queen Street from 1834 to 1874 and George Kenning, publisher and ribbon maker at 16 and 16a). Long Acre was well known for its carriage making businesses, Crosse & Blackwell had a factory in the Charing Cross Road area from the 1830s and Combe's Brewery was located near Shelton Street.

In 1843 the Theatre Regulation Act abolished the patent theatres' (Drury Lane and Covent Garden) monopoly over dramatic and musical performances. This encouraged the building of many new theatres and music halls in the West End of London, which would eventually hold total audiences of 300,000 who also needed refreshment at restaurants and pubs, thus creating a new 'industry' for the Covent Garden area. Great Queen Street acquired its own theatre. Originally the Novelty Theatre in 1882, it later became the Great Queen Street Theatre (under the management of freemason William Penley) and from 1907 the Kingsway Theatre. The English premieres of Ibsen's *The Doll's House* (1889) and Synge's *Playboy of the Western World* (1907) were both staged there. The theatre was damaged by enemy action in 1941 and later demolished.

Memorial to the 1862 Building Committee.

The Victorian Freemasons' Hall

Following the work of Soane and Hardwick, the Great Queen Street site had become a conglomeration of buildings surrounding Sandby's Hall. In 1859 John Havers, a surgeon and the President of the Board of General Purposes, set up an Estates Committee which was, ostensibly, to identify all the property owned by Grand Lodge in Great Queen Street and what income was being obtained from it. However, Havers also used the Committee to provide evidence of a need for a new headquarters in which distinction would be made between those areas used for Masonic meetings and the eating and drinking facilities of the tavern. In his report to the Board Havers stated:

'It appears to me a disgrace and reproach that the most ancient, influential and by far the most wealthy Grand Lodge in the world should longer permit its headquarters to be used as a Tavern.'

Havers was appointed Chairman of what became known as the 1862 Building Committee which embarked on a comprehensive rebuilding of the site. The work of this Committee was aided by further purchases of property in Great Queen Street. Nos 64 and 65 Great Queen Street were acquired in 1848 and 60 and 59 were purchased in 1856 and 1858 respectively. The financial position was improved when the last Tontine nominee died in 1862 which meant that the annual dividend of £250 no longer needed to be paid.

In the rebuilding Soane's Temple would be demolished but Sandby's Hall retained to be used solely for Masonic purposes. Recognising the growth in the number of lodges and in the administrative arrangements required, four lodge meeting rooms were to be built for the increasing number of lodges meeting in the area and accommodation was to be provided for the Grand Master, office accommodation for the Grand Secretary and his staff, a Committee Room, a Library and Morning/Reading Room and offices for the three Masonic charities (the Royal Masonic Institution for Girls [RMIG], the Royal Masonic Institution for Boys [RMIB] and the Royal Masonic Benevolent Institution [RMBI]). The Tavern would comprise a large banqueting hall and 11 other dining rooms of various sizes with kitchens. It would retain its own entrance from the street but there would also be direct access from the new building. The Masonic area and the Tavern would be made architecturally distinct.

The cost of this was estimated at £35,000-£40,000 with furnishing and 'incidental charges' costing a further £3,000-£5,000. The 1862 Building Committee had the benefit of accumulated surplus funds of £21,000 and proposed to borrow the remainder from the Fund of Benevolence at a rate of four per cent interest (said to be less than if they borrowed elsewhere) to be paid back with-

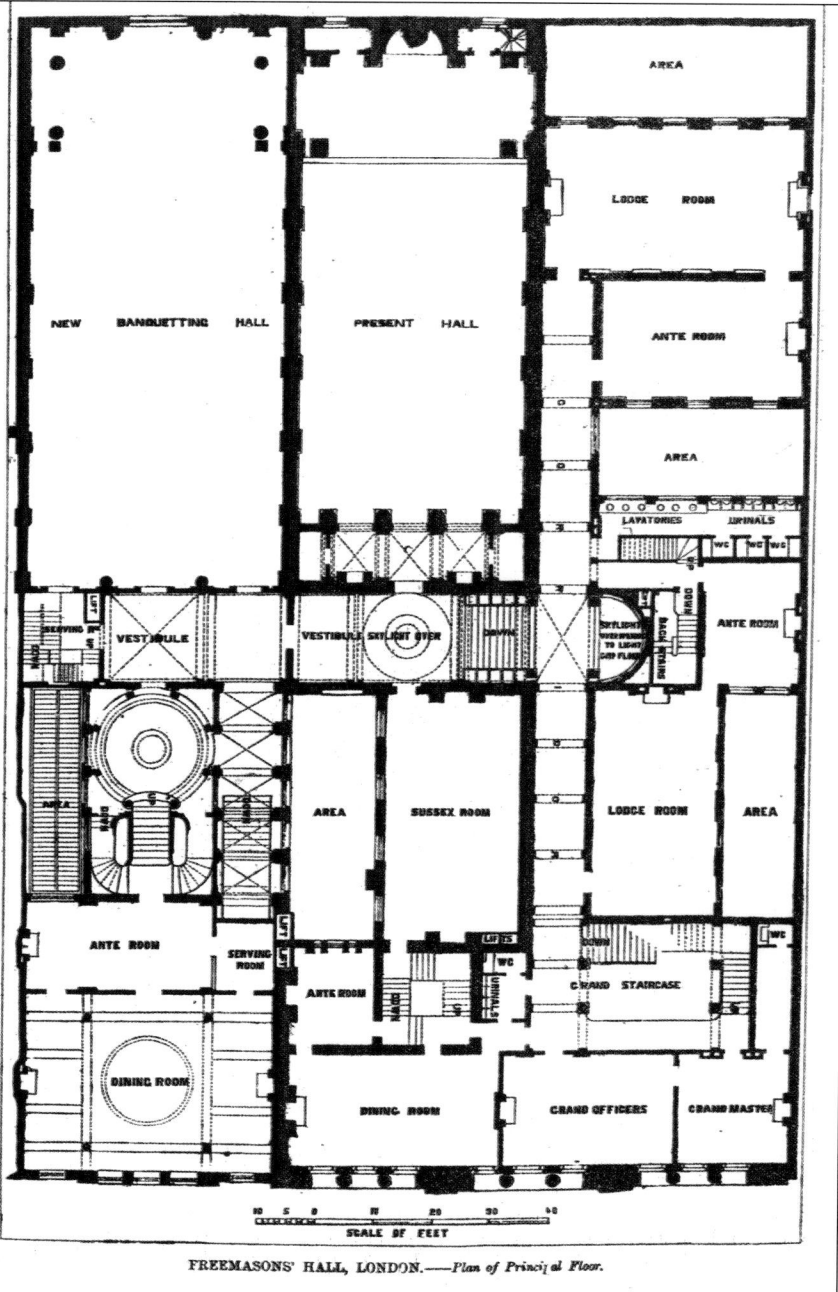

F. P. Cockerell's plan for the Hall and Tavern.

One of the roof trusses for the Banqueting Hall being constructed off site.

John Havers.

in 10 years. Havers estimated that additional income would accrue from a higher rent paid by the Tavern (£500-£600 a year), hiring out the lodge rooms and subscriptions of 10 shillings and six pence (52½p) paid for use of the Library and Reading Room. The Committee added in a report of May 1863 that they 'believe [that] when the really magnificent accommodation which will be afforded becomes generally known — when it is known that lodges and chapters will find in every respect suitable and dignified accommodation, and when it is generally understood that not only our London Brethren, but those from every part of the world will find a Masonic Home of which they may be fairly proud, and which is provided with every requisite comfort, and is open to them at all hours, that the returns will probably far exceed the amount which they have at present ventured to calculate on'.

Architects were invited to forward designs and plans in open competition in early 1863. The directions including the following instructions: 'the Committee expressly notify to competing architects that elegance and simplicity, rather than elaborate ornament in the general character of the designs and economy in the entire cost of the buildings will materially influence the selection'. Applicants to the competition were requested to submit the designs anonymously but with a motto affixed to them accompanied by a 'sealed letter bearing the same motto, and containing the name and address of the author'. Thus the name of the successful architect would only be revealed once a winning design had been chosen. The first placed design was to be awarded £150, the second best £100 and the third placed entry £50.

There were 19 entries to the competition and there was much deliberation as to which design should be declared the winner. The designs were also exhibited for a short time at St Martin's Hall on Long Acre to enable members to view them. Several individuals wrote detailed evaluations of the entries stating their preferences and offering opinions as to which designs should be awarded prizes. An article discussing the merits of several of the designs even appeared in the journal *The Builder* (reprinted in *Freemasons' Magazine and Masonic Mirror* 6 June 1863), a journal that reported on developments in the building trade and often included accounts of new buildings. The Building Committee could not reach a unanimous decision so the architects, James Thomas Knowles and Philip Charles Hardwick, the son of Philip Hardwick, the former Grand Superintendent of Works, agreed to help judge the contest for a fee of 20 guineas (£21). They selected as the superior design the one marked 'L'union fait la force' with the scheme marked 'Stability' in second place and in third place the design marked with a double triangle with the motto 'Blue upon red'. Their opinion was in line with that of the Building Committee with the exception of the third placed design, as the Committee had preferred the plans marked 'Experientia'.

The entry that came second was the work of Edward M. Barry, the son of Sir Charles Barry, architect of the Houses of Parliament. Barry had already undertaken other buildings in the area including the Covent Garden Theatre and the St Giles National Schools in Endell Street. The third

The 1869 Steward's jewel.

Photograph of the exterior designed by Cockerell.

Reverse of the 1869 Steward's jewel.

Thomas, 2nd Earl of Zetland.

placed entry was that of the incumbent Grand Superintendent of Works, Samuel Daukes. As well as being the architect of the almshouses at Croydon built for the Royal Masonic Benevolent Institution, Daukes had considerable experience in hospital building including the lunatic asylum at Colney Hatch, Hertfordshire.

The chosen design, 'L'union fait la force' (meaning 'unity provides strength'), was submitted by the architect Frederick Pepys Cockerell (1833-1878), son of the architect Charles Robert Cockerell and a pupil of Philip Charles Hardwick, one of the additional judges. In his design Cockerell placed the Masonic buildings to the west side of the Tavern, for reasons of light, space and access. The front of the Masonic portion was to 'convey externally an idea of an internal hall'. In his scheme he proposed four alternatives for the appearance of the frontage. The first scheme included an 'arch in the centre of the construction', the arch as Cockerell expounded being 'essentially a Masonic emblem'. He further explained, 'the groups above the four main piers represent four Masonic virtues . . . charity, unity . . . ([characterised by] a figure binding together a sheaf of rods) — wisdom, and fidelity. Around the arch are the signs of the zodiac. Above it, also over the entrance door, and in the frieze between the columns are other Masonic emblems'. This design for the façade was later carried into execution with the figures sculpted by William Grinsell Nicholl (1796-1871) who was particularly known for his architectural sculpture and had earlier worked on the pediment of St George's Hall in Liverpool.

In the Tavern portion of the design Cockerell placed the great dining hall 'upon the same level as the present Hall'. In his plan Cockerell considered the best way to proceed in the order of the construction so 'that the business

The reception of HRH The Prince of Wales (later Edward VII) as Past Grand Master in Sandby's Hall on 1 December 1869, painted by S. Rosenthal.

of the tavern should not suffer'. He suggested that the new kitchen be built at the same time as the Masonic parts. The kitchen fittings could be transferred during the month of September 'when there is no business . . . and the present dining rooms would then be available during the building of the new ones'. Once the Masonic portion was largely complete the Masonic frontage and the library were to be built.

The design also explained how the buildings would be lit and heated and contained a description of the materials to be used and the mode of construction. He estimated that the total cost of the work would be £38,681.

Despite his links with Philip Charles Hardwick, John Havers and the Building Committee were a little uncertain as to Frederick Cockerell's professional capabilities partly due to his youth as he was only thirty at the time. Cockerell therefore procured testimonies from, as he put in his letter, 'a few of the leading members of . . . [the] profession'. The architect Sydney Smirke, architect of the Reading Room in the British Museum, wrote of Cockerell 'that there is no young member of the profession more likely to produce a fine and original work of art than Mr F. Cockerell'. Another leading architect of the period, Sir William Tite, wrote 'that in your father's great knowledge and well deserved reputation, you're (sic) long education under him and from my knowledge of your practical acquaintance with architecture, it [is] impossible to conceive you are unequal to any part of your profession — whether as a matter of taste or of practical execu-

The carpet made for the Hall.

tion and matters of business'.

Once satisfied with Cockerell's capability and having interviewed Cockerell who agreed to modify and improve his design, in June 1863 'it was resolved unanimously [by the Building Committee] that Brother Cockerell be . . . appointed the architect, to prepare the improved plans and designs and to carry out the work on the intended buildings'. Cockerell had not been a freemason when he entered the competition but he was swiftly initiated (in Westminster and Keystone Lodge No 10) in April 1863 and was appointed Grand Superintendent of Works in the same month.

Having appointed an architect the Building Committee looked to select a builder to execute the proposed works. Tenders were sought and the lowest proposal was submitted by Thomas Rider of Union Street, Southwark. He offered to carry out the work for £24,170. Rider's tender was duly selected and a contract was drawn up and signed on 24 December 1863.

Preliminary works began the following week and they soon faced early problems, which as Cockerell reported 'unavoidably retarded progress'. The problem was caused by the 'looseness of gravel . . . chiefly caused from great infiltration from the drains of the tavern'. Correcting the problem cost an extra £437. Such unforeseen problems and additional costs were a feature of the construction and meant that the new hall and tavern took five years to complete.

Although initial work began in December 1863 the foundation stone ceremony did not take place until April 1864. As with the laying of the foundation stone for Sandby's Hall in 1775, the day was

Photograph of Sandby's Hall taken before 1883 by Bedford Lemere.

Jewel and collar of the Grand Superintendent of Works.

Decorative scheme prepared by Sir Horace Jones for the reinstatement of Sandby's Hall after the 1883 fire.

rich with Masonic ceremonial and hundreds of brethren applied for tickets. Having assembled in the Temple (the name now often used to denote Sandby's Hall) those attending proceeded in pairs to a semicircular tiered platform. The ceremony began with a prayer. The inscription on the stone was read by the Grand Secretary, and a parchment copy together with coins of the reign was deposited by the Grand Treasurer in a cavity in the stone. The stone itself was laid by the Grand Master, the Earl of Zetland. An oration was delivered by the Grand Chaplain, Adolphus Woodford, and the ceremony concluded with a procession back to Sandby's Temple. The subsequent banquet supplied by the tenants of the Tavern premises was attended by 400 diners. *The Era* reported that the banquet was 'provided in Brothers Elkington and Shrewsbury's best style, consisting of every delicacy the season could afford, and gave general satisfaction'.

The building was constructed in five different stages in order to minimise disruption to the Tavern's business and by 1865 good progress had been made, enabling the Grand Secretary's Office to move into the building on 1 May. It was also from this date that lodge meetings began to take place in the new accommodation using a temporary entrance to the Tavern whilst the façade was being erected.

The buildings were finally ready to be inaugurated in April 1869. There had been no need for a special fundraising campaign as the Building Committee had used surplus funds and a loan as anticipated by Havers. However, the inauguration was an opportunity for the issue of a commemorative jewel. At the meeting of Grand Lodge in December 1868 it was announced that 'the Grand Master [Thomas, 2nd Earl of Zetland] proposes to name a certain number of stewards for that occasion [the inauguration], and to invite the Lodges generally to send others, and he intends, if it meets the wishes of the stewards, to cause a jewel to be struck, and to permit the Brethren who may serve as stewards to wear the jewel'. The Grand Master nominated 20 stewards, 80 were nominated by lodges and a further 27 were the Grand Stewards for the year. Each paid a fee of six guineas (£6.30) and was presented with a jewel for his services. The jewel was made by Joseph Shepherd Wyon and Alfred Benjamin Wyon, both members of the distinguished family of medallists and consisted of a device suspended from a ribbon. The device was an ornamental five-pointed star in silver gilt with a pomegranate between each of the points, except at the top, where there was an Earl's coronet. On the obverse of the device was a bust portrait in relief of the Earl of Zetland. On the reverse of the device was the façade of the second Freemasons' Hall in relief, with its inauguration date above (14 April 1869) and the Latin motto of the United Grand Lodge of England below. Each jewel was inscribed with the name and lodge name and number of the steward.

The *Freemason's Magazine and Masonic Mirror* reported on the inauguration of the new Hall on 14 April as the 'great event which . . . for so long a period [had] occupied the attention of the entire Masonic Craft of Great Britain . . . It was celebrated in a manner commensurate with the interest which has been manifested in reference to it. The large hall was completely filled by members of the

Decorative scheme prepared by Sir Horace Jones for the reinstatement of Sandby's Hall after the 1883 fire.

Craft from all parts of the kingdom, and the brilliancy of the scene is without a parallel in the history of Masonic proceedings'. Following a procession through to the 'Great Hall', a special meeting of Grand Lodge heard a short address from John Havers concerning the origins and completion of the building, concluding that 'he had carried out the dearest wish of his heart, in the separation of tavern accommodation from Masonry, for they then possessed a fitting temple for the practice of their art, and long might it flourish'. In the oration delivered during the ceremony, Robert Simpson recalled an earlier ceremony: '. . . on Thursday, May 23rd 1776, this hall was dedicated in solemn form, and handed down to us by our brethren of that day as a rich inheritance. And here we stand, at the distance of nearly a century, to renew and enlarge this building in a manner worthy of this later age and more suited to our increased numbers and requirements'. The inauguration concluded with a banquet that, it was reported, 'was provided in a beautiful manner, and reflected the highest credit upon Brother Gosden, the energetic manager of the Freemasons' Tavern Company'.

Once complete, the entrance to the Masonic part of the building was in the centre of the façade. The entrance led to a hall and spacious staircase lit by a domed light. A corridor from the hall gave access to administrative offices and also to offices for the charities. This enabled the RMIG and the RMIB to relocate from 16a Great Queen Street. The RMBI had been based in the Grand Secretary's office. The library and the coffee room reserved for members were located at the front of the building. The front rooms on the first floor were for the use of the Grand Master and the Grand Officers. The remainder of the floor consisted of two large lodge rooms along with anterooms and access to Sandby's Hall. Located on the second floor were more lodge rooms and the third floor was reserved for living accommodation

Decorative scheme prepared by Sir Horace Jones for the reinstatement of Sandby's Hall after the 1883 fire.

for the servants of Grand Lodge and also for those of the Tavern. The basement floor included rooms for the individual who held the Masonic office of Grand Tyler and general storerooms.

The Tavern's main feature was the large banqueting hall, its proportions being 96ft (29.5m) by 43ft (13.2m) and 45ft (13.8m) high and decorated in the high Baroque style. Directly underneath the banqueting room was a kitchen of the same area. There were also further smaller dining rooms and halls and it was reported in the journal *The Builder* in 1866 before the completion of the construction work 'it is believed that no building in London will offer such large accommodation for public entertainments'.

The distinction between the Tavern and the Masonic building was visibly achieved and can still be seen through the design of the adjoining façades, which although they harmonised in their Classical style, were distinct, with the Portland stone façade of the Masonic portion and the red-brick (now painted) of the Tavern. *The Builder* commented that 'the front displays considerable originality, and there is much elegance in the details. We must congratulate Mr Cockerell on his achievement.'

As a mark of thanks to John Havers and the other members of the Building Committee a 'sculptured tablet . . . with an appropriate inscription, to be surmounted by a marble bust of the Chairman . . . and surrounded by marble medallion portraits of the members of the Building Committee' was erected in recognition of their work. Joseph Durham, a respected sculptor of the period who had worked in the studio of Edward Hodges Baily, agreed to carry out the commission for 300 guineas (£315). Once complete, the testimonial was situated in a prominent position on the first floor landing of the main staircase of the new Freemasons' Hall. After the construction of the Masonic Peace Memorial Building in the 1930s it was relocated near the Board Room.

In 1875 Cockerell received correspondence from the archaeologist Henry Maudslay who had undertaken excavations for the Palestine Excavation Fund near the walls of Jerusalem during which he had uncovered a quantity of mosaic pavement. Maudslay offered to donate this as decoration for flooring in the new building. Forty-seven cases were duly received and the mosaic laid in the vestibule leading to Sandby's Hall in 1877. A decorative panel that formed part of this floor was subsequently retained in the later Masonic Peace Memorial Building and laid outside the Board Room.

Grand Lodge continued to purchase the freeholds of various properties adjoining the new Freemasons' Hall as they became available. Purchases in the late 1870s enabled offices for the charities to be built on the site of one of the New Yard properties. They were designed by John Gibson and built at a cost of £2,500 with a muniment room in the basement costing a further £450. John Gibson (1817-1892) was known particularly for his designs for bank buildings. He was initiated in Earl Spencer Lodge No 1420 in 1873 and was Grand Superintendent of Works from 1879-81.

On the night of 3 May 1883, Sandby's Temple was badly damaged by fire. The *Freemasons' Chronicle* reported 'shortly before midnight, a fire was discovered at the Freemasons' Hall . . . and by the time the fire engines arrived, the elegant hall known to Craftsmen as 'the Temple' was completely destroyed'. In the fire the portraits of the past Grand Masters on the walls of the room were completely destroyed and the roof collapsed. The cause of the fire was 'proved to be through a beam which was in too close proximity with the passage of a flue from the adjoining Tavern'. The rest of the building was largely unaffected.

Sandby's Hall had been left largely untouched in Cockerell's work apart from some repairs. Further growth in membership and in the number of lodges had made it apparent for some time by this date that his Hall did not provide enough accommodation for all those who wished to attend meetings of Grand Lodge. The fire provided an opportunity to consider whether a new, larger Hall could and should be built. Sir Horace Jones was the Grand Superintendent of Works at this time. He was Architect and Surveyor to the City of London, responsible for the markets at Smithfield, Billingsgate and Leadenhall, for the Griffin Memorial marking the site of Temple Bar and for Tower Bridge. Immediately after the fire the Premises Committee even considered whether to relocate Freemasons' Hall entirely to a riverside site at the Adelphi, south of the Strand, reflecting concern with the slum conditions around Great Queen Street. The idea was rejected as the freehold of the site was not available. Jones reported that the cost of refurbishment of Sandby's Hall could be met from the proceeds of the insurance claim. He also considered a scheme to extend Sandby's Hall by taking in the Banqueting Hall of the Tavern. A Special Building Committee was appointed which included Sir John Monckton, town clerk to the City of London, John Gibson and George Burt, one of the partners of the contracting firm John Mowlem. The Committee held discussions with Spiers & Pond Ltd, the lessees of the Freemasons' Tavern, and with Thomas Bacon, of Bacon's Hotel (64 and 65 Great Queen Street). This Committee put forward a plan, in line with the scheme Jones had considered, to demolish Cockerell's Banqueting Hall to enable a larger temple with 1,500 seats to be built on its site. Bacon's Hotel would be acquired and substantially refurbished as replacement banqueting facilities. The Committee suggested that this new Temple could be built for £40,000. Despite the expertise of the Committee members, their proposal met considerable criticism from other members of Grand Lodge, led by an ailing John Havers who expressed scepticism about the cost. Plans for enlargement were abandoned in favour of reinstatement, the cost of which was, as envisaged, covered by the proceeds of the insurance claim. This had been completed by May 1884 allowing for some minor alterations to Sandby's Hall to provide 100 extra seats, improved fire exits and a new system of ventilation. Copies of the portraits were made by a number of artists including Louis William Desanges, a member of Globe Lodge No 23 and Lodge of Friendship No 6 and a former Grand Steward, and B. S. Marks, a member of St David's Lodge No 979 (now No 679), Aberdare, and Buckingham and Chandos Lodge No 1150.

Part of the mosaic originally laid in the vestibule outside Sandby's Hall.

Freemasons' Tavern

From their earliest years, Masonic lodges met in the back rooms of inns and taverns and eating and drinking (and singing and music making) were important elements of their meetings. Originally eating and drinking probably took place during Masonic ceremonies but it later became customary for the members of the lodge to dine afterwards. The development of freemasonry in the early 18th century had coincided with the growth of coffee houses which provided secular meeting places for business and pleasure and which often served food. The Hall Committee considered that the provision of catering facilities rented out to an innkeeper was a means of generating income for Grand Lodge. In December 1774 it was agreed to let the back house on the site where Sandby was building his Hall to Luke Reilly to be used as a coffee house and tavern. Reilly paid £25 per annum for the use of the premises but was eventually asked to surrender his lease in 1787.

After Sandby and Tyler's rebuilding (see above), the new premises were leased in 1790 to Michael Richold (or Richbold) and John Mollard, described as wine merchants. The Hall Committee was able to purchase the leasehold of the house adjoining the tavern to the east late in 1790. A new kitchen for the Tavern was built behind it and the house itself leased to Richold and Mollard. It was a difficult time to build up a business as Britain was shortly to embark on an extended period of war with revolutionary France (and later Napoleon). Despite Richold and Mollard's claim in a memorial to the Hall Committee in January 1794 that 'they have brought the tavern from a state of obscurity into considerable repute' and rent increases being waived, profits remained insufficient and they gave up their tenancy in 1801 citing in a further communication with the Hall Committee 'the nature of the times (which) . . . has made a great alteration in the profits of . . . our . . . business'.

An attempt was made to run the Tavern by a group of 'Subscribers' but by 1805 the Tavern had closed. John Bayford and Sir Williams Rawlins, who were both members of the Hall Committee, were appointed to conduct the affairs of the Tavern and negotiated a new lease from 1808 with Robert Christopher Sutton, William Thorn and

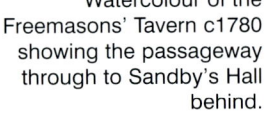

Watercolour of the Freemasons' Tavern c1780 showing the passageway through to Sandby's Hall behind.

John Jackson Cuff. All had business experience. Thorn had been the headwaiter at Canonbury House and Cuff had once been an apprentice to Richold and Mollard at the Tavern but was at the time running a small eating-house in Drury Lane. Sutton owned the Highbury Barn tavern and was able to provide capital. When Sutton and Thorn retired Cuff took over the operation assisted by Hoggary, his chief clerk and Arnold, his head cellarman, both of whom seem to have participated in a profit-sharing scheme that meant that they each had an estate worth more than £1,000 when they died. His son John Cuff joined his father in the business in 1827 and John Jackson Cuff retired to run another inn, The Old Ship, at Brighton in 1834. On his retirement his tradesmen held a dinner in his honour and presented him with a candelabra. When he died in November 1848, he left a fortune of more than £120,000 and his death was marked with a lengthy obituary in the *Freemasons' Quarterly Review* in 1849.

Further evidence of the profitability of Cuff's Tavern is that in 1815 Cuff purchased the two houses adjoining the Hall to the east (62 and 63) and allowed Soane to build his Temple in the gardens behind them. He subsequently sold the houses to Grand Lodge in 1838 at no profit, receiving an inscribed silver tea urn worth 50 guineas (£52.50) in return.

From 1839 Cuff's former clerk, Thomas Bacon, a member of the Lodge of Regularity since 1832, became joint proprietor of the Freemasons' Tavern with John Cuff. He was later sole proprietor but became insolvent in 1851 and was replaced by William Watson, Thomas Coggin and Benjamin Banks. Their business similarly failed to prosper and more new tenants, Shrewsbury & Co (David Shrewsbury, James Thomas Cookney and George Goode Elkington), took over in 1856 at a lower rent. Shrewsbury and Elkington were both Northamptonshire masons and had been members of Pomfret Lodge No 360 since 1837. When they moved to London Shrewsbury joined the Lodge of Regularity (now No 91) and Elkington joined Royal Somerset and Inverness Lodge No 4 and later St John's Lodge No 167 in Hampstead. Bacon continued as the proprietor of Bacon's Hotel (64 and 65 Great Queen Street).

Major changes occurred in the 19th century that altered the experience of eating out in London and affected the nature of business of the Freemasons' Tavern. Restaurants, often run by French or Swiss Italian entrepreneurs such as Daniel Nicolas Thevenon at the Café Royal, Pagani's in the Strand (1874), Oddenino's and Frascati's, were established setting higher standards with French haute cuisine and allowing for mixed dining by both men and women. The catering industry became more commercialised which introduced additional capital and companies such as Spiers & Pond (see below) could build larger, more elaborate restaurants which could offer a wide range and price of meal. The first companies to build hotels in London were the railway companies building near their termini (such as the Charing Cross Hotel at the western end of the Strand in the 1860s) but others soon joined this trend. The Westminster Palace opened in 1860, the Langham Hotel (Portland Place) in 1865 and the Savoy Hotel in 1889. The new hotels offered food and accommodation and tried to emulate the standards set by hotels in Paris and New York. The contemporary *Langham Hotel Guide* described this approach as being 'an attempt . . . to introduce the best points of the three systems, English, French and American, the comfort of the first being amalgamated with the elegance of the second and the discipline and organisation of the third'. All these new venues meant that there were more places to cater for the growing number of lodges (the Café Royal was one of many that had its own lodge room) thus competing with the Tavern.

Following this trend towards commercialisation, a new company was formed in 1864 for 'the purchase of the lease, goodwill, and stock in trade

John Jackson Cuff commissioned distinctive plates and bowls in blue and white ceramic decorated with a transfer print of the Tavern.

The reverse of the plate showing Jackson's name.

Jewel of the Lodge of Regularity No 91, a lodge to which many of those connected with the Tavern belonged.

of the Freemasons' Tavern'. The prospectus for the new company proposed to raise £65,000 by the sale of shares and explained how 'for nearly a century . . . the Grand Hall' had been used to hold 'great public meetings of a large number of the political, religious, and educational societies' and that the existing tenant (David Shrewsbury was closely involved with the company) would continue to take an active part in the management of the business of the Company. It took over the tenancy in 1865 but it did not prosper despite employing the former royal chef Charles Francatelli as manager from 1870 to 1876.

In 1877 Alfred Best took over the tenancy from the Freemasons' Tavern Company Limited but soon assigned his lease to Spiers & Pond Limited. They also purchased the lease of Bacon's Hotel in 1883. Formed by Felix Spiers and Christopher Pond, both Englishmen, as a successful catering business in the Australian gold fields and responsible for taking the first English cricket team to Australia, Spiers and Pond came to London in the 1870s where their business expanded. They built the Criterion Restaurant and Theatre at Piccadilly Circus in 1874 and also catered at the Gaiety Theatre Restaurant and the Theatre Royal, Drury Lane. The Company was the subject of a comic song, *Fanny and Jenny* by W. S. Gilbert which compared them with their rival caterers, Bertram & Roberts. Felix William Spiers had become a freemason in Australia (Australia Felix Lodge No 697) in 1856. In London he joined the Grand Masters Lodge No 1 in 1876 and remained a member until 1908.

After the rebuilding of the site in the 1860s Sandby's Hall was reserved for Masonic meetings. The Tavern continued to be a venue for the meetings of numerous bodies including the Artists Benevolent Fund. In 1888 a meeting was held there to establish the Lawn Tennis Association, continuing a tradition of links with sporting associations which included the Football Association formed at the Tavern in 1863.

Despite their considerable experience, Spiers and Pond were unable to make the hotel business viable and surrendered their lease in December 1888. Grand Lodge received an offer to operate the business as a temperance hotel but took up instead an alternative offer, at a slightly higher rental of £360 pa for a 49-year lease, from another Masonic body, the Grand Lodge of Mark Master Masons, who also undertook to spend about £3000 converting the building into their new headquarters with a Masonic temple, lodge rooms, office accommodation and dining for 150 people.

Spiers & Pond's lease on the Freemasons' Tavern was due to expire in 1905. Little improvement had been made to the Tavern in the previous 40 years and the standard of food and facilities was attracting much criticism as highlighted by Frank Richardson, Grand Director of Ceremonies at the Grand Lodge meeting in March 1905: 'the Tavern is so badly constructed, the kitchens in the wrong place and no sufficient lifts, that it is utterly impossible for any restaurateur to supply good dinners in the place'. Neither Grand Lodge nor Spiers & Pond were willing to pay for the necessary improvements. In March 1905, the Board of General Purposes announced that it had invited five 'well-known restaurateurs' to tender for the lease. As well as Spiers & Pond, these were Holborn & Frascati Limited, the proprietors of the Café Royal, J. Lyons & Co and Auguste Oddenino, proprietor of the Imperial Restaurant and a member of Covent Garden Lodge No 1614. The Board wanted the lease to include provision for a limited number of lodges to provide their own wines and only pay corkage. This proved unacceptable to most of those approached and negotiations proceeded only with J. Lyons. The Board had, however, agreed to spend up to £30,000 on reconstruction of the Tavern and its redecoration.

Further plans were then developed to extend the Tavern by taking over the adjacent premises in Middle Yard and Wild Court that increased the cost of the project by £20,000. However, by early

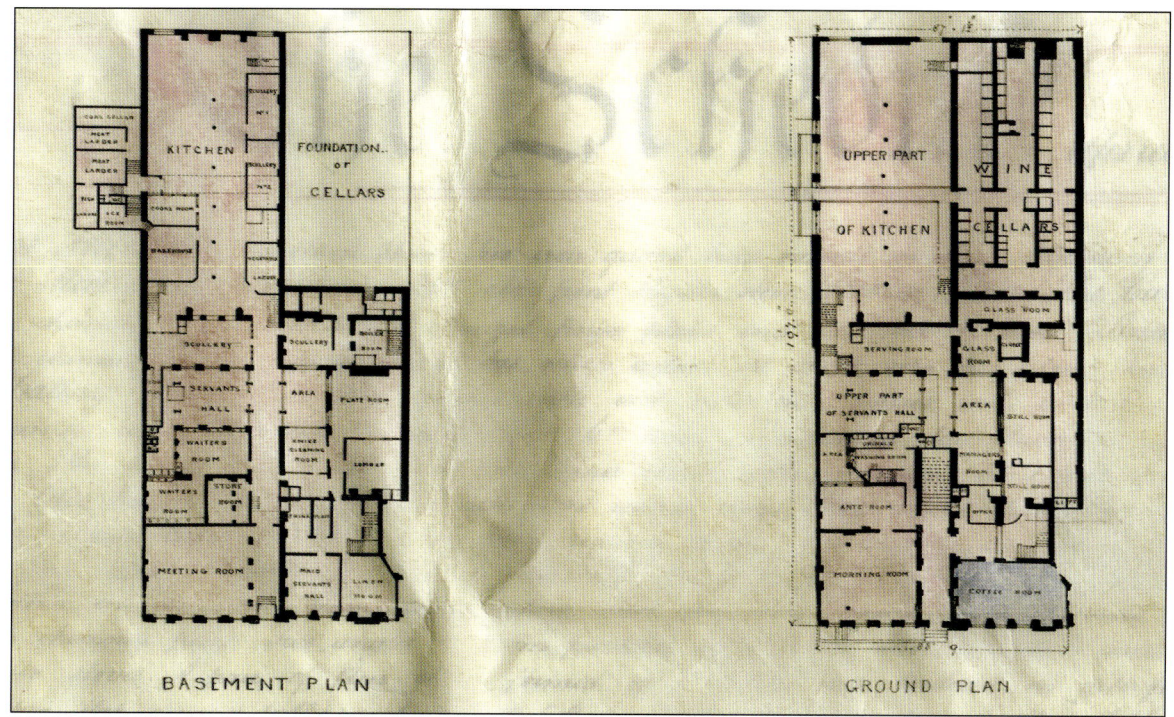

1906 negotiations with J. Lyons had collapsed over the extent to which the Board was willing to make additional payments for trade fixtures and fittings. With the Tavern having been closed since June 1905, Grand Lodge was facing a loss of income and also undermining the future viability of the business (and any income) by forcing lodges to make alternative dining arrangements. A Special Committee was appointed to examine the whole question of the future Tavern premises and it set about negotiating a new lease. There were no satisfactory responses to an advertisement for tenders and further negotiations with restaurateurs were also unsuccessful.

Finally, in order to resolve this situation, in March 1909, Grand Lodge decided to spend the £30,000 required to put the Tavern premises in proper order including the demolition of property in Middle Yard. The work, which included rebuilding the kitchen and enlarging the Banqueting Hall, was completed by the end of the year. To mark this new era the name of the Tavern was changed to the Connaught Rooms in honour of the Duke of Connaught and Strathearn who was the Grand Master at the time and agreement was reached with the Connaught Rooms Limited to take on a new lease. The Managing Director of the company was George Harvey and, under his leadership, the premises once more became a successful venue. Harvey, former manager of the Hotel Cecil in the Strand, had been initiated in Capper Lodge No 1076. He was to become a member of a number of other lodges and was later a borough councillor, member of the London County Council, Mayor of Holborn and Member of Parliament for Kennington. He was knighted in 1936. His son succeeded him as Managing Director of the Connaught Rooms Limited.

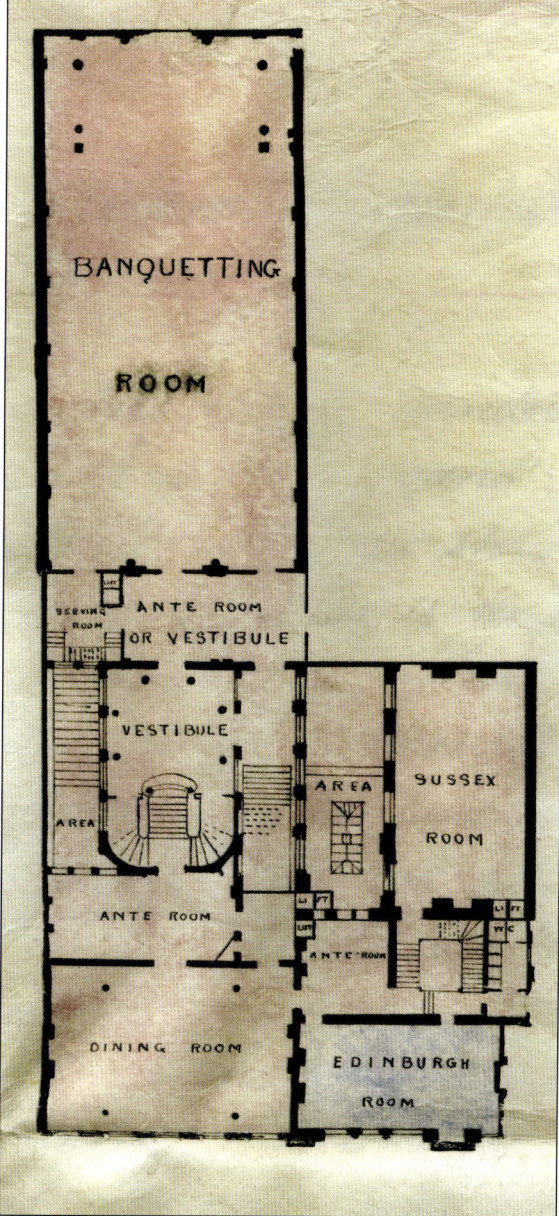

Plan of the Tavern remodelled by Cockerell, showing the vaults underneath Sandby's Hall.

The cover of a brochure published in 1910 to mark the opening of the Connaught Rooms.

The main staircase of the Connaught Rooms in 1910.

Modern photograph of Cockerell's Banqueting Hall.

Great Queen Street and its Environs in the 20th Century

On 18 October 1905, King Edward VII officially opened Kingsway, a new road linking the Strand with Euston station, which was the largest road building scheme in London since the construction of Regent Street in 1820. It resulted in the clearance of one of the most overcrowded areas of late Victorian London and the removal of 3,500 residents. Kingsway, a broad tree-lined avenue, was designed not only to improve north–south connections but also to create an impressive highway suitable for London as an imperial capital. The new road was over 60ft wide. Its prestige was such that it was expected that it would be lined by impressive office buildings, hotels and theatres which were built gradually during the first 20 years of the century. No new pubs were allowed (although 51 had been demolished as part of the scheme). Kingsway had a tunnel for an electric tram as motorised transport was increasingly replacing horse-drawn vehicles. Transport links were also extended by the electrification of the underground railway which enabled the system to operate at a deeper level. The Central Railway opened in 1900 running between Marble Arch and the Bank of England in the City with a station at the junction of High Holborn and Kingsway whilst the Piccadilly Line (1906) ran underneath the Great Queen Street site with stations at Covent Garden and Holborn.

Despite the failure to gain approval for any rebuilding in the 1880s, continued growth in membership exacerbated the accommodation problem. The RMIG moved its offices to a building on the north side of Great Queen Street in 1906 and the RMIB moved to 34 Great Queen Street. Grand Lodge continued to purchase property on the south side of the street. To the west numbers 57 and 58 were purchased in 1880 but were tenanted and Grand Lodge could not secure vacant possession until 1899 when both the houses were demolished. A new wing was designed (by Henry L. Florence) to match that of the Tavern so that the buildings formed a balanced and symmetrical whole. This new building which cost about £12,000 provided improved space for the Library and Museum of Grand Lodge (the first dedicated space) and also comprised a new Committee room, lodge rooms and greater accommodation for the Assistant Grand Secretary and other Grand Officers. Florence, who was Grand Superintendent of Works from 1898 to 1905, had worked in the office of F. P. Cockerell on the 1860s Hall and later with Lewis Isaacs designed a number of hotels including the

Jewel of Kingsway Lodge No 3027 showing the new road.

The cover of a guide to the Borough of Holborn (c1905).

Holborn Viaduct, the Carlton and the Coburg. He had been a member of Westminster and Keystone Lodge No 10 from 1883.

The last two houses to the west before New Yard (55 and 56) were acquired in 1899 for £8150. Both were tenanted properties with leases that expired in 1913.

In 1908-9 Grand Lodge established a Building Fund based on a levy of 6d per annum (2½p) on each member. By 1913 £20,000 had accumulated in this Building Fund. A Committee had been established to decide the form of a Memorial to Edward VII, Grand Master 1874-1901, who had died in 1910 and in December 1913 it proposed that the memorial should take the form of an extension and improvement of Freemasons' Hall including further office accommodation and lodge rooms and 'the building of a fine Library and Museum' which was to be called the Edward VII Memorial. Assuming the income from the levy continued at the existing rate it was claimed that the estimated cost of £40,000 would be covered by the Building Fund by 1919 so that there would not be any need for a special appeal. In 1913-14 plans were drawn up to demolish numbers 55 and 56 and build the extension on that site and on part of New Yard (purchased in 1914). However, 56 Great Queen Street had once (1786-8) been home to James Boswell who may have written part of his biography of Dr Johnson there and there was a commemorative plaque on the house marking this. Nos 55 and 56 had once formed part of Bristol House and were said to be the only two houses in Great Queen Street which retained any part of the original 17th century elevations. The oak staircase in 55 Great Queen Street was also of this date and was decorated with carvings of oak leaves, oak apples and acorns. The proposals to demolish these buildings attracted the attention of the incipient building conservation movement including the Society for the Protection of Ancient Buildings. Leading campaigners such as Lord Curzon as President of the Committee for the Survey of the Memorials of Greater London and Arthur Evans, the archaeologist of Crete and President of the Society of Antiquaries, wrote to protest.

Alexander Burnett Brown, the Grand Superintendent of Works, investigated whether the façade of the two houses could be retained and incorporated into the extension but the structures were deemed too dangerous to do this. Sir Laurence Gomme, a member of London County Council Lodge No 2603 who, as Clerk to the London County Council, had promoted the commemorative plaque scheme and had written the historical sections of the Council's *Survey of London* for the area, suggested the solution: that the balustrade of the staircase and a portion of the façade be removed and donated to the Geffrye Museum. Work on demolition and building the extension commenced early in 1915 but proceeded slowly. The manpower required by the armed forces of the 1914-1918 War caused labour shortages. Work continued slowly until 1917 when the new building had been made weatherproof but was then stopped when the workforce was withdrawn by the Ministry of Munitions. The extension was never to be completed and was demolished for the Masonic Peace Memorial Building.

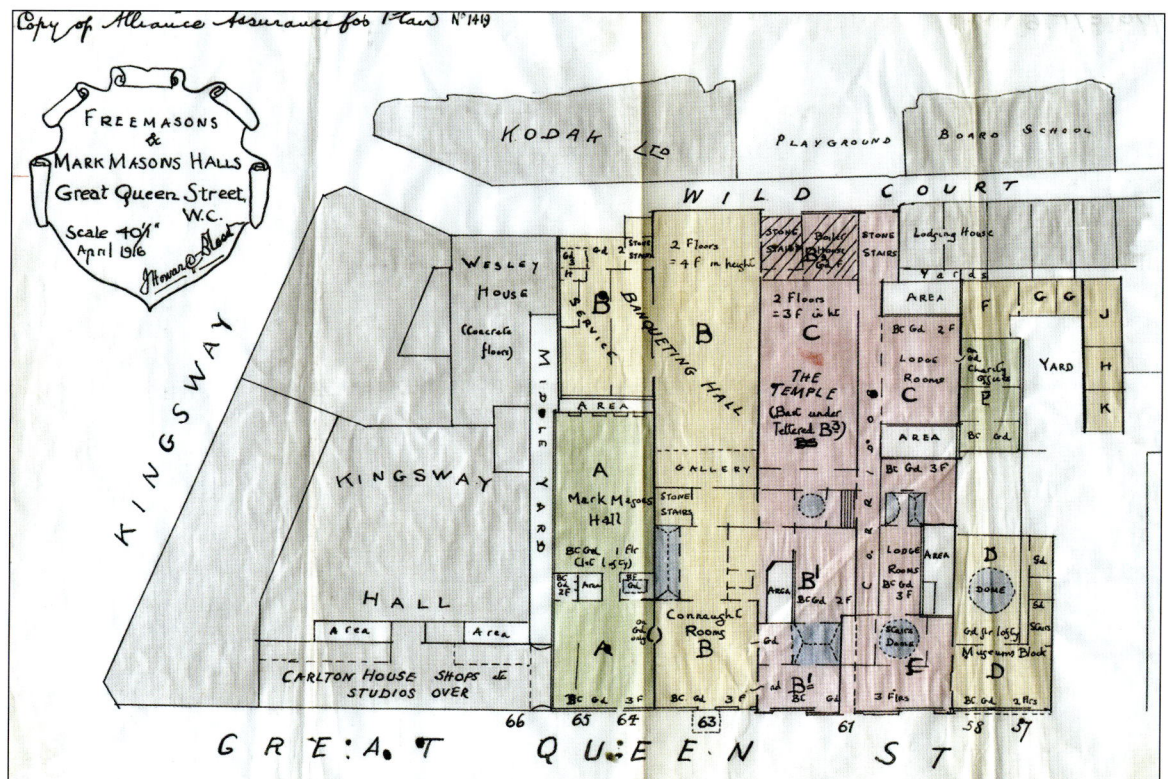

Top left:
Jewel of the Covent Garden Lodge No 1614, showing one of the market buildings.

Above:
The extension designed by Henry Florence in 1900.

Plan of the Great Queen Street site, showing the 1915 extension.

55-56 Great Queen Street shown in 1904. *Reproduced with the permission of the Camden Local Studies and Archives Centre*

48 Great Queen Street, one of the last properties on the south side of the street to be purchased by Grand Lodge.
Reproduced with the permission of the Camden Local Studies and Archives Centre

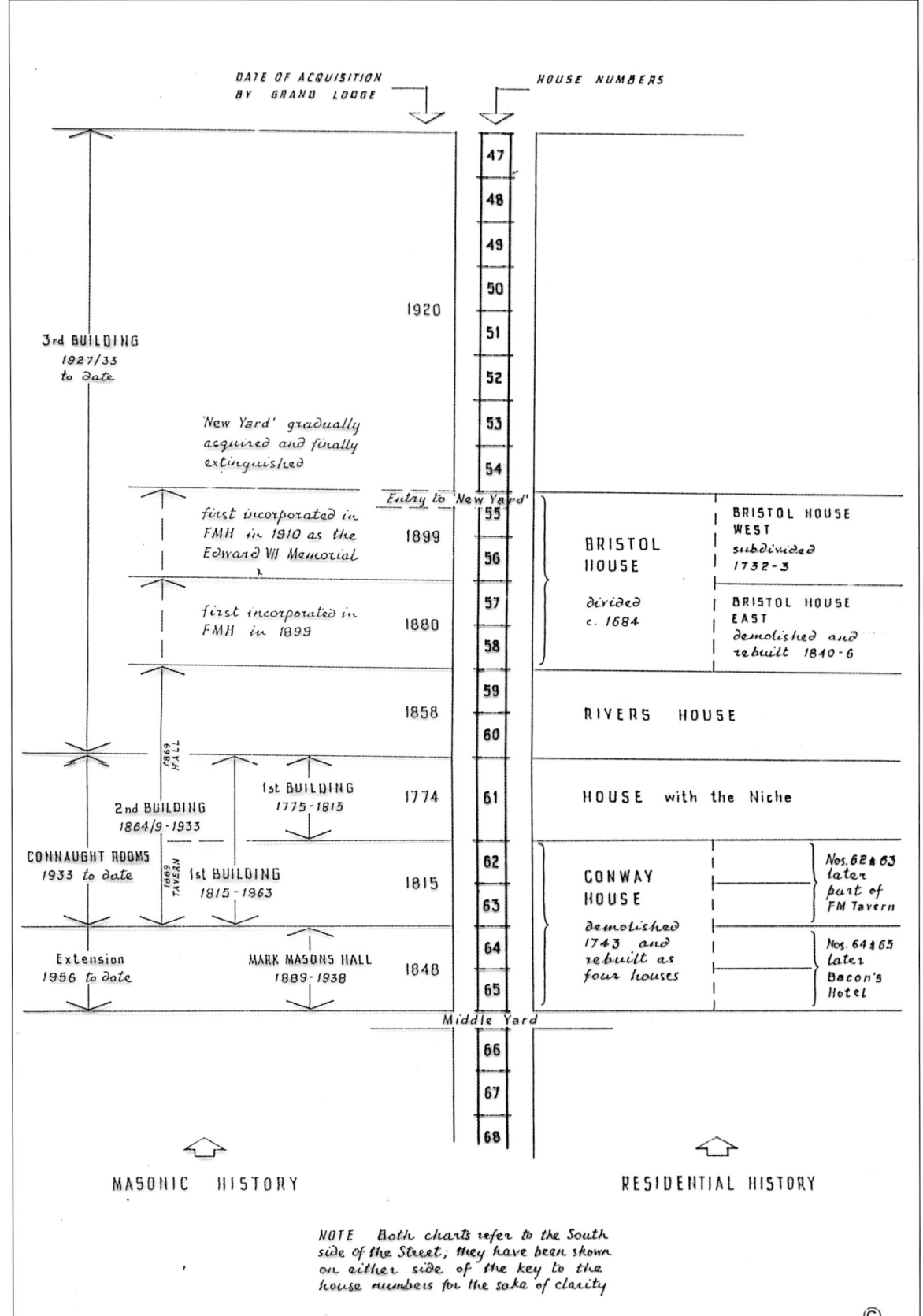

Plan showing the progressive extension of the Great Queen Street site. *Reproduced with the kind permission of T. O. Haunch*

The Library and Museum

Both the Premier Grand Lodge and the Antients Grand Lodge had maintained registers of their members since the end of the 18th century and both retained important correspondence. These records were generally kept in secure boxes (several are recorded as being made), presumably, in the case of the Premier Grand Lodge, in one of the rooms maintained for the use of the Grand Secretary and the various committees. The Articles of Union of 25 November 1813 referred to depositing the new great seal of the United Grand Lodge 'in the archives' but at this time Grand Lodge had few other treasures apart from the portraits of the Grand Masters hung on the walls of the Hall, some chairs, a bible and the Ark of the Masonic Covenant which were used in meetings of the Grand Lodge. A proposal to consider 'the mode of forming, preserving and regulating a Masonic Library and Museum' was agreed by Grand Lodge on 6 September 1837 following a report by the recently installed Grand Superintendent of Works, Philip Hardwick, concerning the possible use of the houses at 62 and 63 Great Queen Street. With this additional space available for expansion, it was announced in Grand Lodge on 7 March 1838 that 'the room on the ground floor and on one side of the passage in the House No 63 appears to be well calculated for the present purposes of a masonic Museum and Library' and that, 'a sum of money not exceeding £100 be placed at the disposal of the Board [for] the purpose of providing for the reception of books, manuscripts and objects of Masonic interest, and for commencing the formation of the Library and Museum'.

Dr Robert Crucefix made the first donation of a bound four-volume set of *The Freemasons' Quarterly Review* and a call for more donations resulted in William George Turner, a Past Master of Strong Man Lodge (then No 53) and Mount Lebanon Lodge (then No 87) depositing 80 volumes. Grand Lodge appointed the two Grand Secretaries as ex-officio curators and by 1840 the Library consisted of 250 books and two manuscripts.

Despite the initial interest, progress in creating a Library and Museum was slow. One of the junior clerks in the Grand Secretary's office, Arthur Loutherbourg Thiselton, himself a keen collector, spent some time in this first Library and Museum. His obituary in the *Freemasons' Quarterly Review* in June 1842, described his work: '. . . he arranged the few books and manuscripts in the Masonic library, and had the contributions to this depart-

Dr Robert Crucefix, an early supporter of the Library and Museum.

ment been ever so extensive, he would have been delighted to have regulated them; as it was, he considered the office of curator as disgraceful, having nothing to do.' A move at Grand Lodge in 1847 by John Royston Scarborough, a Poplar wine merchant and member of Mount Moriah Lodge, supported by Robert Crucefix, to secure an annual £20 grant to the Library and Museum was withdrawn after a speech from the Grand Master, the Earl of Zetland suggested that £20 was not enough and they would need a Librarian '. . . of great skill and high education to be constantly on the premises . . .' who would cost £150 per year which was more than Grand Lodge could afford. Scarborough's action prompted the Board of General Purposes to report on the state of the collections. It

Henry Sadler, the first Librarian and Curator, shown here in 1879 as Grand Tyler.

The Museum in 1900.

noted that the Library owned 279 books on freemasonry and other subjects, a series of printed lists of lodges and calendars dating back to 1723, some Court Directories and six atlases. Of the £100 grant, only £56 9 shillings and 6 pence (£59.47$^1/_2$) had been spent. For whatever reason the Library and Museum's premises in No 63 were no longer available or adequate and the Board recommended moving the Library into the anteroom of Soane's Temple. The first Library regulations were proposed including regular opening times with the Library open on Tuesdays, Thursdays and Saturdays from 2pm until 8pm, readers being required to sign a visitors' book, a rule that no books should leave the Library and that the Grand Tyler should be in attendance to deliver books to readers and return them to the shelves, for which he would receive an extra £15 a year. It was also proposed that a Library catalogue should be produced from the remainder of the £100 grant, to be sold to members at 6d (2$^1/_2$p) and that the *Quarterly Communication* of Grand Lodge should note when the Library was open and invite more donations. Scarborough welcomed the report believing that '. . . great good would be conferred on Masonry by the Library' and its recommendations were passed. Some of these regulations remain in force today.

In their plans for the redevelopment of the site, the 1862 Building Committee had proposed the creation of a Coffee Room and Library that was to be available to subscribers on payment of an annual fee. This attracted few subscribers despite the publication of a printed catalogue by Henry Hemsworth, a member of Oak Lodge No 190 and of the Board of General Purposes. Despite little indication of usage of the Library and Museum in the 1870s, in June 1880 Grand Lodge agreed to give the Library and Museum an annual grant of £25 to be spent on preservation, binding and acquiring further books.

It was the appointment in 1887 of the Grand Tyler, Henry Sadler, as Sub-Librarian, which inaugurated a period of major change for the Library and Museum. Although the Grand Secretary was still ex-officio Librarian and Curator, Sadler's salary was increased by £20 per year to attend the Library and opening hours were extended to 10pm on Mondays and Thursdays. Sadler was an excellent choice. He organised and collected archive material and used this as the basis for much of his own research. He was also a member of Quatuor Coronati Lodge No 2076, the first lodge of Masonic research. The Masonic historian Robert Freke Gould said of Sadler '. . . scarcely a single Masonic book would have been written without the author being assisted by him'. Sadler retired as Grand Tyler and was appointed full time Librarian and Curator in 1910 with an annual salary of £150, the sum the Earl of Zetland had suggested in 1847. He died just a year later. He had produced two catalogues of the Library collection in 1888 and 1895. The latter is almost double the size of the former, giving some indication of the growth of the collection during his time. The formation of the research lodge in 1884 and the growth in Masonic historiography supported by Sadler's work greatly increased interest in the Library and Museum and the collection of Masonic artefacts and books. Lists of donations and acquisitions to the Library and Museum started to appear in the *Quarterly Communication* from 1893. The collections continued to grow and could be displayed properly for the first time in the new extension of the Hall created by Henry Florence after 1900.

The rules for the architectural competition for the design of the Masonic Peace Memorial Building in 1925 included instructions to provide for space for a substantial Library and Museum incorporating a gallery, two Librarians' rooms, a workroom, two strong rooms, a large museum space with good lighting and a separate reading room. Ashley and Newman's winning design placed the Library and Museum on the first floor of the building on the same level as the ceremonial areas. This space, where it has remained, enabled the Library and Museum to grow into one of the largest Masonic collections in the world.

The Library in 1900.

The Library area in the Masonic Peace Memorial Building.

Top: A recent view of the Museum.

Above: Exhibition about the work of the photographer and freemason Alvin Langdon Coburn held at Freemasons' Hall in 2002.

Publicity leaflet of the Library and Museum Charitable Trust which has been responsible for the Library and Museum since 1999.

The Masonic Million Memorial Fund

On 27 June 1919 an Especial Grand Lodge was held at the Royal Albert Hall to celebrate the peace after the 1914-1918 War. The Grand Master, the Duke of Connaught, was unable to attend due to illness but a message was read expressing his hope that the opportunity would be taken:

'. . . to create a perpetual Memorial of its [ie the Craft's] gratitude to Almighty God . . . [to] render fitting honour to the many Brethren who fell during the War. I desire that the question of the Memorial be taken into early consideration . . . The great and continued growth of Freemasonry amongst us demands a central home; and I wish it to be considered whether the question of erecting that home in this Metropolis of the Empire, dedicated to the Most High, . . would not be the most fitting Memorial.'

At the next meeting of Grand Lodge in September it was proposed that a Special Committee be appointed to take forward this idea. The man appointed to be Chairman of this committee, Sir Alfred Robbins, had been President of the Board of General Purposes since 1913, a position he was to hold until his death in 1931. Initiated in Gallery Lodge No 1928 in 1888 (Master in 1902), he was a leading journalist as the London correspondent of the *Birmingham Post* for 35 years and an early member of the Parliamentary press lobby. For his services to freemasonry he was often referred to as the 'Prime Minister of Freemasonry'. Robbins had also been closely involved with the various prewar plans and appeals and was under no illusion about the magnitude of the task that he described as 'a very great effort' and 'not a matter of tinkering but of temple-building'. An important feature of any new appeal would be that it would be made to all members and it would be voluntary.

In January 1920 details of the appeal to raise £1,000,000 were distributed to lodges. Via their lodge each individual member received a facsimile copy of a personal letter from the Grand Master, a copy of the scheme details and a subscription form. The letter included the first use of the appeal's name: the Masonic Million Memorial Fund. It was originally proposed that contributions to the Fund would be marked by a range of awards representing different levels of donation, including certificates and medals with various motifs. However, the complexity of this met some criticism and a revised scheme was put in place whereby individual members who contributed at least 10 guineas (£10.50) were to receive a silver medal and those who contributed 100 guineas (£105) or more, a gold medal. Lodges that contributed an average of 10 guineas per member were to have their names recorded in the new building as Hall Stone Lodges and the Master of each such lodge was to be entitled to wear a special medal as a collarette. In addition a Province or District jewel was awarded for donations by a province or district of an average of 500 guineas (£525) per Lodge. Only three of these jewels were ever awarded. They were for one province, Buckinghamshire, and two districts, Burma and Japan. In recognition of their contribution lodge rooms in the completed building were later named after them. At a later stage a fifth jewel was introduced

The Special Collectors' jewel.

Four examples of the Hall Stone jewel.

Sir Alfred Robbins, President of the Board of General Purposes 1913-31.

known as a special collector's jewel for those members who raised a list of contributions of at least 250 guineas (£262.50). By the end of the appeal 53,224 individual medals had been issued and 1,321 lodges had qualified as Hall Stone Lodges. The running of the Fund became an enormous task and involved large amounts of paperwork, including individual record cards logging the amount and timing of each member's donation (which could be made over a period of years), handled by the Grand Secretary's office.

One design used was to be for all the medals. In May 1920 a small sub-committee was appointed to organise a competition for designs for the proposed jewel. A prize of 75 guineas (£78.75) was offered. There was a large response but from the many designs received that of Cyril Saunders Spackman was selected. His design included a cross to symbolise sacrifice, the dates of the war commemorated and an Angel of Peace holding a temple to represent the gift of a Temple in memory of those members who gave all for King and Country, Peace and Victory, Liberty and Brotherhood. Spackman (1887-1963) had been initiated in Panmure Lodge No 720, London, in January 1918 (resigned 1923). Later in 1938 he became one of the founders of Beaux Arts Lodge No 5707 meeting at Sutton. The jewel was manufactured principally by Allan Gairdner Wyon, whose ancestors had made the 1860s jewel with others made by J. R. Gaunt.

The first Hall Stone jewel to be awarded was presented to the Grand Master on 1 June 1921. At the same time the first list of 200 lodges that had qualified or notified their intention of qualifying was published and in December 1921 the first presentations were made to Masters of 38 lodges. Each medal was inscribed with the name and lodge number of the recipient (or rank in the case of a Grand Officer) and was presented with a note of thanks and a description of the jewel. Presentations to individual members were made in lodge meetings and to Masters of Hall Stone Lodges at meetings of Grand Lodge. Qualifying lodges were identified in the annual Masonic Year Book. Frequent presentations helped to maintain interest.

Following the tradition of Masonic charities it was decided to hold a fundraising event. In order to encourage as many members as possible to take part and to make the event special, it was decided to stage a single event— a lunch at Olympia. That lunch, held on Saturday, 8 August 1925, still holds the record for the largest sit-down meal. Special trains were laid on to transport members to the venue. Over 7,000 members were fed five courses and coffee, served by 1,250 waitresses in just over an hour! Five miles of tables were laid with 50,000 plates, 30,000 glasses, 30,000 knives, 37,000 forks and 15,000 spoons. The diners enjoyed salmon, lamb, chicken garnished with tongue and York ham. A central conning tower was erected in the

Laying the Foundation Stone for the Peace Memorial Building at the Royal Albert Hall.

gallery which was fitted with electrical signalling devices for the caterers to supervise the event. There was also a loudspeaker system with amplifiers that allowed all the diners to hear the speeches clearly. Music was provided by the band of the Welsh Guards. Books of matches were issued to diners at the end of the meal featuring an image of the event jewel on one side and the coat of arms of the United Grand Lodge of England on the reverse. Cigars and cigarettes packed in specially designed cases were also distributed.

A Festival Steward Jewel was issued, designed by John Angell, a member of Medway Lodge No 1678, Tonbridge. Two versions exist — one to be worn by all those who attended this meeting with an S indicating a steward and one without an S which was made available later to all those who had qualified to attend but had been unable to do so.

At the end of the lunch, the Grand Master was able to announce that the funds received (or committed) to the appeal had reached more than £825,000.

With fundraising now sufficiently advanced to enable commitments for the new building to be made, the next event in the fundraising campaign was the ceremony to lay the foundation stone. In order to accommodate as many spectators as possible (8,000), the ceremony was to take place at the Royal Albert Hall on 14 July 1927 with the real stone simultaneously laid on site assisted by telegraph. Attendance at the Royal Albert Hall was restricted to those who qualified by their contributions to the Fund as a further encouragement for contributions. The stone itself was provided by Lodges 2, 4 and 12 as the surviving founding lodges of Grand Lodge in 1717; the cement was provided by the Grand Lodge of Montana 'to cement the bond of brotherly love' and the Grand Master used the Wren Maul, once used (in the opinion of its owners, the Lodge of Antiquity No 2) to lay the foundation stone of St Paul's Cathedral.

In 1930 it was agreed that the levy established in 1909 and paid by every member in England and Wales towards the Building Fund should cease with effect from January 1931. The Building Fund, which stood at £170,000 would be 'devoted towards the erection and decoration of the new Grand Temple and its surroundings as a Memorial' to Edward VII.

A further fundraising event was the Dedication of the building itself in 1933 when, once again, qualification to attend was dependent on contributions to the Fund. Over 12,000 applications for tickets were received. The ceremony was held on 19 July 1933 with an Especial Grand Lodge the previous day at the Royal Albert Hall to celebrate the event. The Dedication ceremony took place in the new Grand Temple and was relayed to the other Lodge rooms in the building. After the service the Grand Master toured the other rooms and gave a short speech in each. By the end of that year, total contributions made to the Masonic Million Memorial Fund were £979,000.

Specific financial contributions were made for furniture and decorative features including the bronze doors of the Temple from the Provincial Grand Lodge of Lancashire, Eastern Division, a new Grand Master's throne, contributed by the Provincial Grand Lodge of Kent, and the Memorial window in the first vestibule provided by the Provincial Grand Lodge of Shropshire. The cost of furniture and decoration led the Grand Master to make his final appeal on behalf of the Fund in November 1936 for a further £50,000, which was met. An additional £6,000 was also raised for a bronze casket to house the Roll of Honour of those that had died in the 1914-1918 War. In June 1938, the Special Committee made its final report although payments for Hall Stone jewels continued to be made until the end of the year.

Masonic Million Memorial Fund
FESTIVAL

OLYMPIA, LONDON, W.

Vins

Amontillado

Sauterne

G. H. Mumm
Cordon Rouge
1913

Courvoisier's V.V.O.
Liqueur Brandy

Spirits

Perrier

Menu

Hors d'Œuvre Suédoise

Darne de Saumon Ravigote
Ravier de Concombre

Côtelette d'Agneau Victoria

Poulet découpé, Garni de Langue
Jambon de York
Salade Mimosa

Boule de Neige glacée Plombière
Gâteau Mascotte

Café

August 8th, 1925

Menu for the Olympia event.

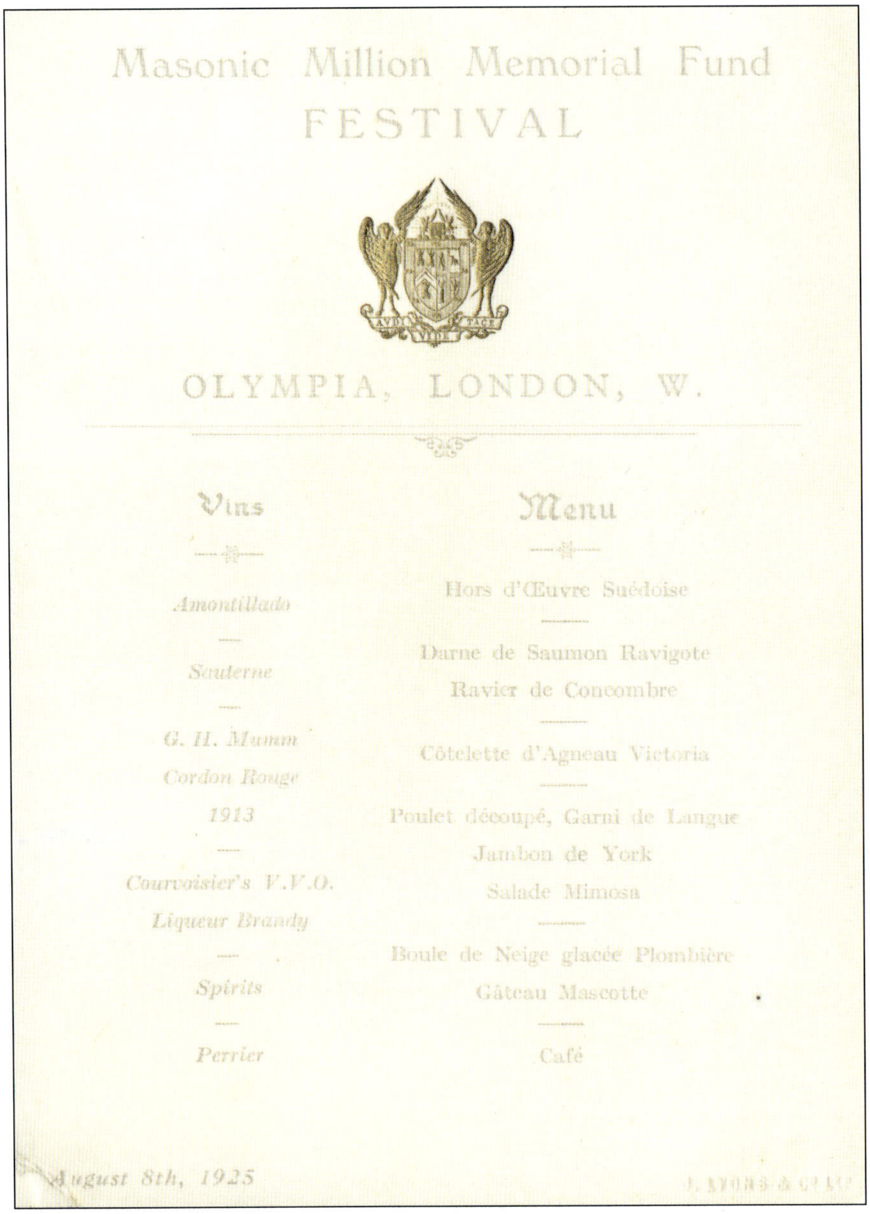

The Committee reported the following statement of receipts and payments:

Receipts

Contributions	£1,043,787
Contributions for furnishing	£11,885
Proceeds of Building Fund	£170,302
Interest on invested contributions less costs of administration	£156,071
Total	£1,382,045

Payments

Building work	£1,172,019
Properties purchased	£164,541
Medals	£27,309
Architects competition, assessors' fees, foundation stone ceremony	£9,508
Cash (subject to cost of Memorial Shrine)	£8,668
Total	£1,382,045

The new building

In 1920 the opportunity finally arose for Grand Lodge to purchase numbers 47 to 54 Great Queen Street, small properties to the west of the existing building bounded by Wild Street and Wild Court. The headquarters of Kelly & Co, publishers of the *Post Office Directory* had been based at 51-52 from 1867 to 1893. The area purchased included New Yard, a public right of way, which involved lengthy negotiations with the local authority regarding its closure.

As the fundraising scheme progressed the Special Committee looked at other possible sites for the new building both in central London and the suburbs. By August 1922 it was agreed that there was only one possible alternative site — the Adelphi Terrace between the Strand and the Thames Embankment. The merits of the two sites were debated at a meeting of Grand Lodge held on 6 December 1922 in the Kingsway Hall and the vote was overwhelmingly in favour of Great Queen Street. The Adelphi site was believed to involve greater cost.

As the fundraising continued, an International Architects Competition was launched through the auspices of the Royal Institute of British Architects in 1925 to design the new building. For the purposes of the competition it was proposed to treat all the properties owned by Grand Lodge on the south side of Great Queen Street as if it were a cleared site including the sites of Mark Masons' Hall and the Connaught Rooms but competitors were instructed that building was to commence on the site between Wild Street and the existing Hall (Sandby's Hall) and sufficient accommodation

was to be provided to replace that of the 1868 Hall (and to accommodate the Royal Masonic Benevolent Institution). A group of assessors were appointed to draw up the conditions of the competition, compile instructions and advise on the selection of the final designs. They were Sir Edwin Lutyens (as President of the RIBA) and two leading freemasons, Walter Cove and Alexander Burnett Brown. The competition was divided into two stages: an initial 'Sketch Competition' and a 'Final Competition'. An extensive list of requirements and plans of the site were sent out to each of the competitors, which detailed the building's requirements, including a Temple, Lodge rooms, library and museum, reading and writing rooms, smoking room and a licensed restaurant. Competitors were required to submit plans and elevations as well as a typewritten descriptive report to explain their designs. The designs were sent in anonymously together with a sealed envelope containing the artist's name and address. Both were numbered but the envelopes with the contestants' details were not opened. Approximately 100 entries were received in the Sketch Competition and from these 10 designs were chosen to move on to the Final stage.

On 6 May 1926 the assessors announced that they had arrived at a unanimous decision that this design submitted by competitor number 109 more closely fulfilled the requirements in the Instructions than any other. Competitor number 109 was then revealed to be Messrs Ashley and Newman. At the request of the RIBA the 10 selected final designs were displayed at its headquarters in Conduit Street. During the eight-day exhibition 656 visitors were recorded.

Henry Victor Ashley (1872-1945) and Francis Winton Newman (1879-1953) had been in partnership since before 1907 when they won their first architectural competition for the extension to the Birmingham Council House. They had a wide-ranging practice designing banks, factories, extensions to hospitals and housing. Ashley was an enthusiastic freemason initiated in St Andrews Lodge No 231 in London in 1910. He was Master of this lodge in 1916 and remained a member until his death. He was also a member of Arts Lodge No 2751, Hiram Lodge No 2416, Sir Thomas White Lodge No 1820 (as an old boy of Merchant Taylors' School) and St Andrews Chapter No 231. He was a founder of Loyal Heath Lodge No 4716 based in Hampstead. Ashley was appointed Assistant Grand Superintendent of Works in 1924 and Grand Superintendent of Works in 1937. Newman was initiated in Arts Lodge No 2751, possibly proposed by Ashley who had joined the lodge the previous month. He was appointed Grand Superintendent of Works on Ashley's death in 1945.

Demolition of the vacant property along Great Queen Street began in March 1927. The extended negotiations regarding the closure of New Yard

H. V. Ashley.

F. Winton Newman.

were completed including an agreement to realign the junction of Great Queen Street, Wild Street, Drury Lane and Long Acre that opened up a vista of the tower of the new building. As work continued with the construction of the steel frame, a detailed photographic record of the project was begun which, together with Newman's architectural drawings, provided illustrations for leaflets distributed to lodges to keep them in touch with the project. Portland stone walls were in place by

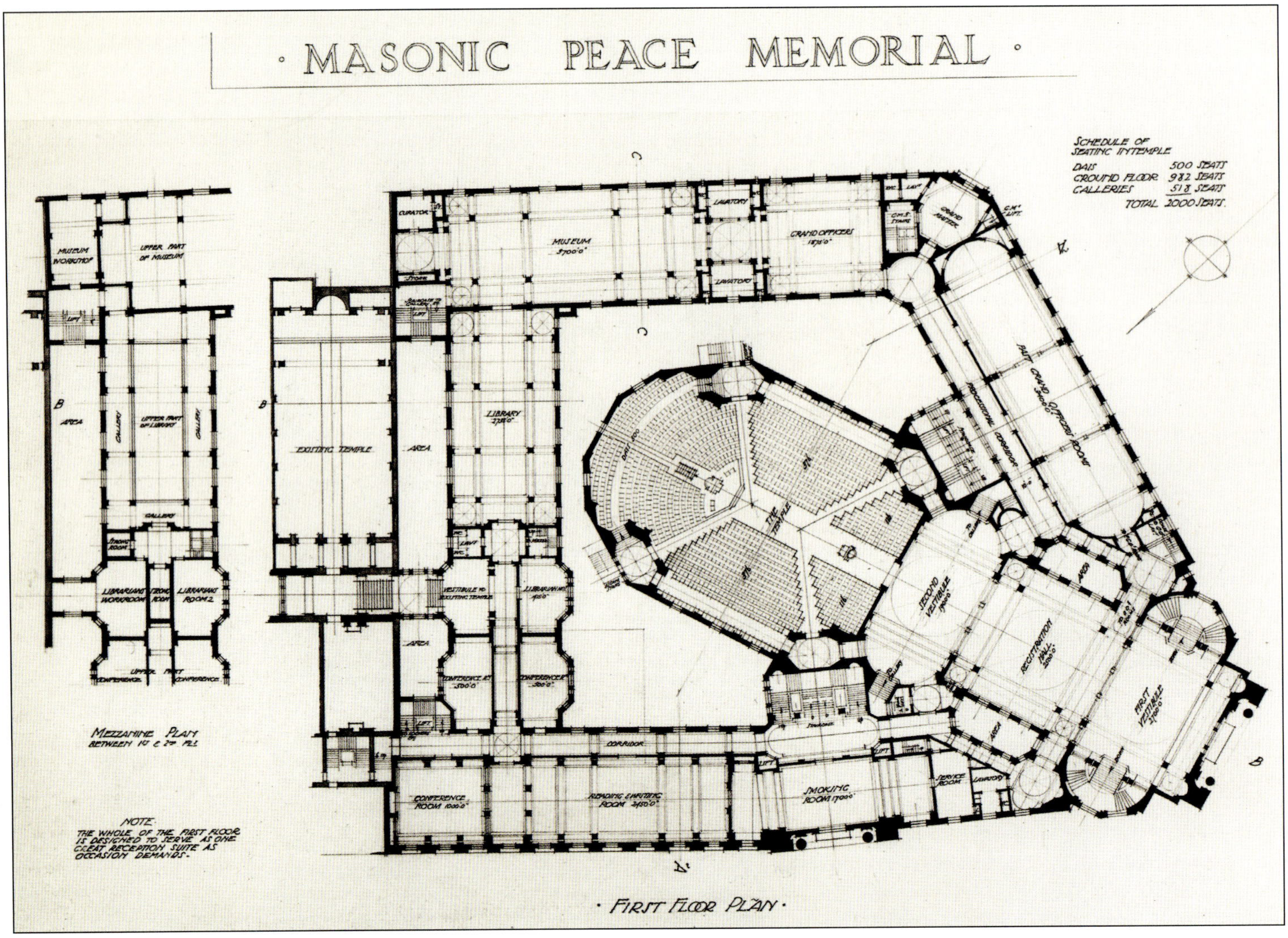

Architects' plans showing Sandby's Hall alongside the new building.

The Great Queen Street site, looking east as demolition began.

One of the vestibules, showing lists of Hall Stone lodges.

The foundation stone of the Masonic Peace Memorial Building.

late 1930. In the summer of 1931, the first six lodge rooms (along the Wild Court frontage) were completed together with temporary accommodation for administrative staff (based in what was to become the Past Grand Officers' Robing Room). The first lodge meeting was held in the new building on 15 September 1931 attended by the Grand Secretary and the Grand Superintendent of Works. The Victorian building was then vacated and demolished.

In March 1932 it was agreed to demolish Sandby's Temple. This had never been contemplated in the original plans but the Grand Superintendent of Works reported serious defects in its structure that became particularly apparent when adjoining buildings were demolished. The architects' plans were adjusted to allow the Connaught Rooms to be extended and the Balmoral Room was built where Sandby's Hall had once stood.

The Connaught Rooms and Mark Masons' Hall were unaffected by the new building although several direct access routes were created to the former from the new Hall. The lease held by the Grand Lodge of Mark Master Masons expired in 1939 and negotiations with Grand Lodge were begun for the renewal of the lease, intending to demolish the existing building and replace it to a design by Ashley and Newman which would be consistent with the design of the Masonic Peace Memorial Building. Demolition began in August 1939 but was quickly curtailed by the outbreak of the 1939-1945 War the following month. Work on the site was abandoned until the 1950s when an extension to the Connaught Rooms was built in 1956.

The tower of the new building under construction, showing the steel framework.

The tower seen from Long Acre before street realignment.

Construction work on the tower.

Ashley and Newman commissioned a scale model of the Grand Temple (right). The Grand Temple as built is show below.

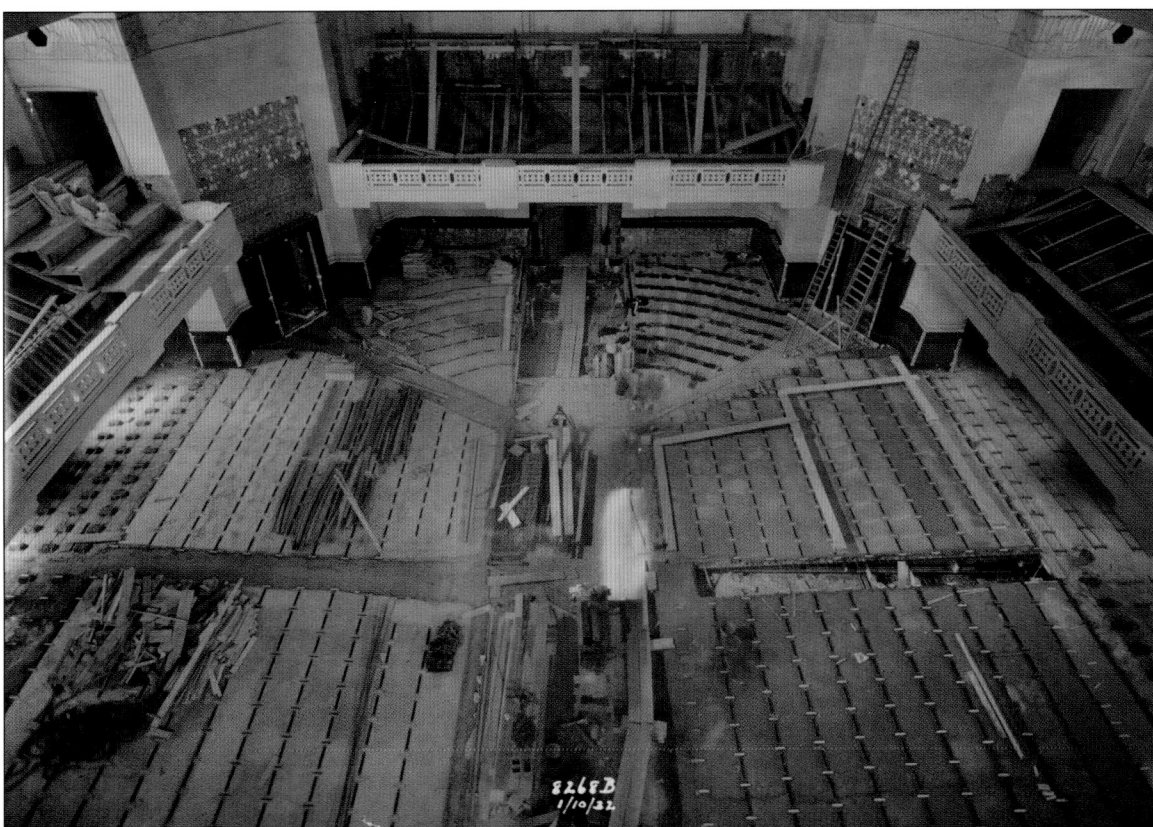

The Grand Temple under construction.

The construction of the mosaic cornice in the Grand Temple.

Craftsman at work on the decoration within the building.

Working on the plaster ceiling of a lodge room.

The Masonic Million Memorial Fund

The Masonic Peace Memorial Building.

THE
FOUNDATION STONE
of the above building will be laid by

FIELD MARSHAL

H.R.H. The Duke of Connaught & Strathearn, K.G.,

MOST WORSHIPFUL GRAND MASTER,

on the afternoon of

THURSDAY, JULY 14th, 1927.

at the

ROYAL ALBERT HALL, KENSINGTON, S.W.7.

(Synchronised by electrical control with the Site in Great Queen Street)

This announcement implies that the Grand Master's foremost wish is now near realisation.

It only remains for the Craft to make one further effort to give the Grand Master the assurance that his Appeal has met with a complete response.

Some information respecting the Fund will be found overleaf.

F S 2.   P.T.O.

Programme for the Foundation Stone Laying.

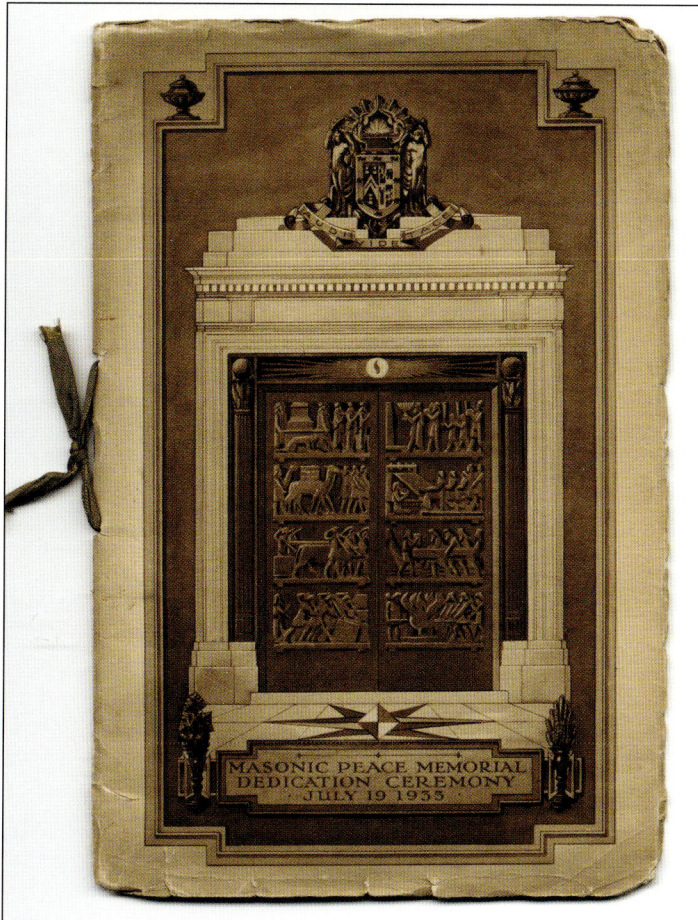

Programme for the Dedication of the building.

COUNTRY LIFE

VOL. LXXIV.—No. 1906. SATURDAY, JULY 29th, 1933. [PRICE ONE SHILLING. POSTAGES: INLAND 1½d., CANADA 1½d., ABROAD 3d.

H.R.H. THE DUKE OF CONNAUGHT

The Duke of Connaught, who performed the dedication ceremony of the Masonic Peace Memorial last week, wears, in this photograph, the insignia of Grand Master of the United Grand Lodge of England, an office which he has held since 1901. His Royal Highness was till then, from 1886, Provincial Grand Master of Sussex.

Country Life magazine in July 1933 pictured the Duke of Connaught, Grand Master, in his regalia and featured an article about the Masonic Peace Memorial Building to mark its dedication.

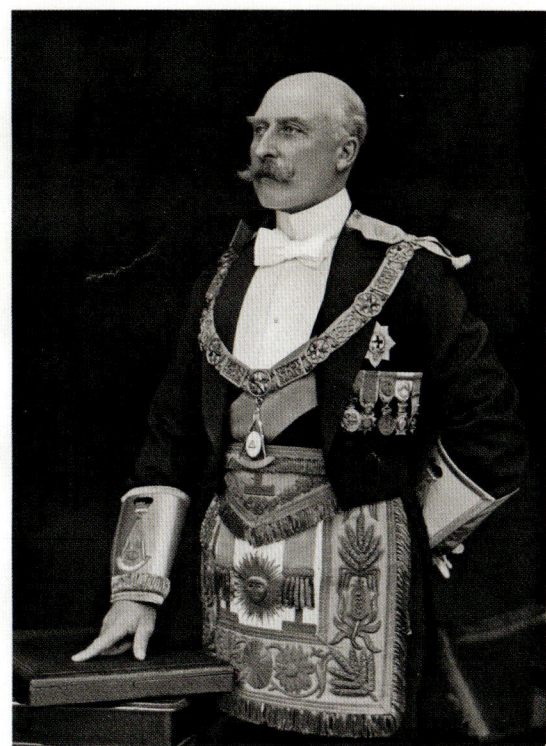

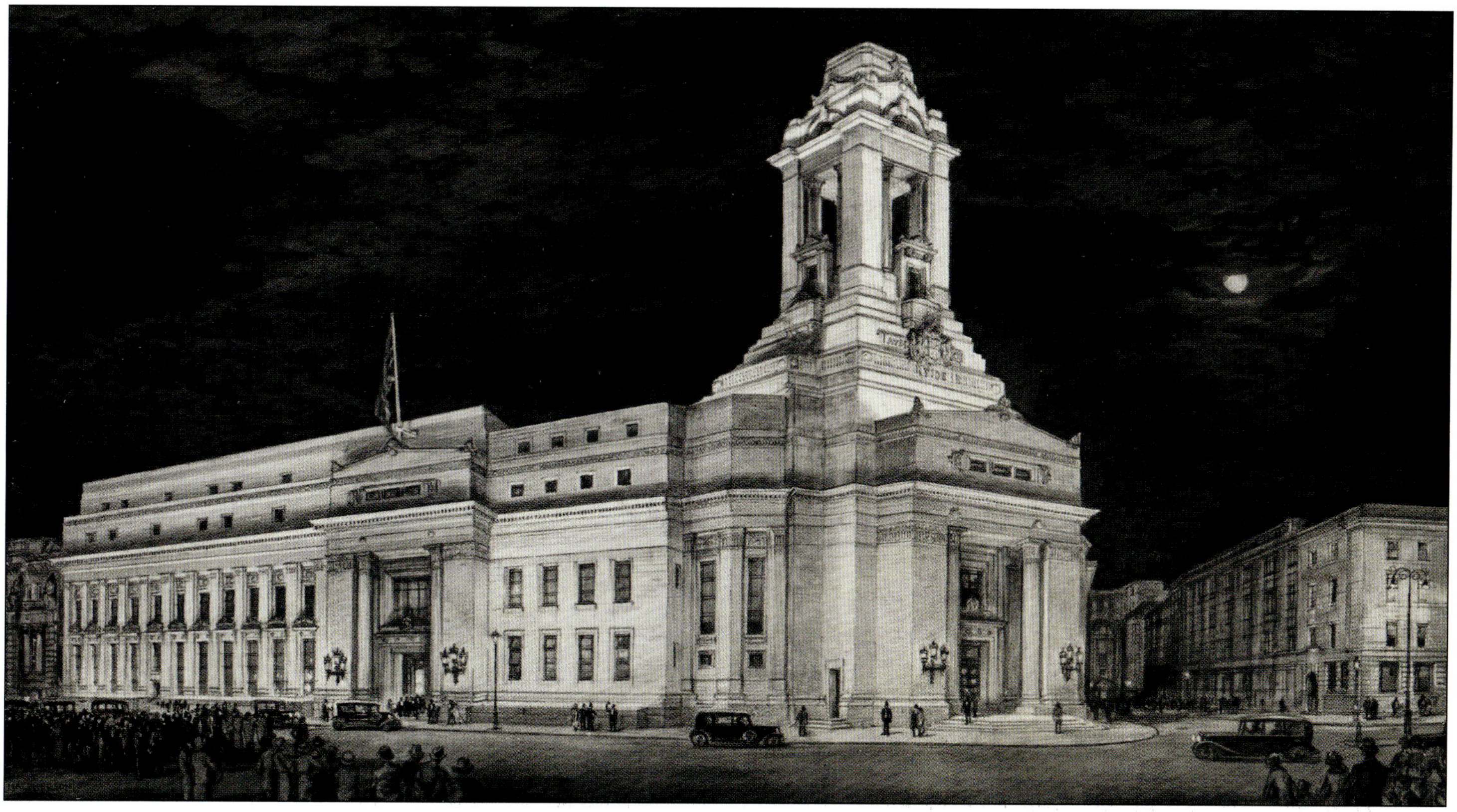

Artist's impression of the Peace Memorial Building.

Despite artists' impressions, views of the new building were restricted by properties on the corner of Drury Lane and on the north side of Great Queen Street.

The Building at War

The likelihood of damage to individuals and property from aerial bombing was well recognised by the late 1930s. Arrangements for the security of the civilian population were increased with the introduction of air raid precautions, digging of shelters in London parks and elsewhere and the development of procedures for evacuation from large cities. There is no evidence that Grand Lodge considered the possibility of evacuating the Masonic Peace Memorial Building (or Freemasons' Hall, as it was also becoming known) and moving the administrative staff to another site outside London. The building not only housed the central administrative function of freemasonry, it also acted as the ceremonial headquarters and as accommodation for the meetings of hundreds of individual lodges. When war was declared in September 1939, lodge and chapter meetings were suspended but this suspension was lifted within a month. Even if the clerical staff could be moved, there would have been no realistic alternative locations for lodges to meet. Moreover many more lodges found themselves meeting at Freemasons' Hall as their usual meeting places were either requisitioned or, later, suffered damage. So Grand Lodge stayed put and began to prepare the building for war.

Protective work was carried out on the roof of the building in 1939 and the skylights, fanlights and other glass were covered over with timber and sandbags. There was always concern about damage by incendiary bombs falling into the courtyards. Protective walls were erected in the courtyards in front of the windows to help protect them. From January 1941 the government and local authorities enforced further arrangements for detecting and combating fires in designated business and industrial areas — the fire watching scheme. There was a fire watching position next to the tower of the building, manned by members of staff who spent one night a week there. Provisions were made on the roof for supplies of water and there were also buckets of sand to put out small fires.

After the fall of France in June 1940 and with the Blitz continuing, measures were taken to preserve some of the most important original Grand Lodge records. The Grand Secretary wrote in October 1940 to his opposite number in each of New South Wales, New Zealand, Massachusetts and Canada asking them to look after details of where important documents were stored:

'Dear Brother Grand Secretary

'We have considered it desirable to place certain of our original documents in a place of safety in order to preserve them for posterity. Should misfortune befall all who are aware of the location, it is desired that the information be made available to their successors.

'It has been decided that a sealed envelope, which is enclosed, be deposited with four Grand Lodges, of which yours is one, asking them to preserve it and return, unopened, upon receipt of a letter making the request, or a cable worded "Return Envelope".

'I feel sure that you will not mind doing this service for us.'

The Grand Secretary of Canada in Ontario replied:

'We gladly accept the trust and assure you that your instructions will be strictly carried out. Let us hope, however, that we will soon receive an "all clear" cable and that victory will be ours.'

When return of the envelopes was requested on 10 October 1945 the Grand Secretary wrote: 'In those days we were very concerned as to the safety of many of our historical records and it was a comfort to know that certain papers were deposited with you.'

Notice of the building's use as a public shelter.

FREEMASONS' HALL, GT. QUEEN ST., W.C.2.	PUBLIC AIR RAID SHELTER.

TELEPHONE NUMBERS.	
CONTROL OFFICER	321
CONTROL OFFICER (DURING RAIDS)	200
FIRST AID POST	263
MAIN ENTRANCE	231
WILD STREET ENTRANCE	289
WILD COURT ENTRANCE	331
TOWER	296
ELECTRICAL	200
DO.	243

Sir Sydney White, Grand Secretary 1937-57.

The basement of Freemasons' Hall in London was one of a number of buildings scheduled as an air raid shelter. It could accommodate 2,500 people in the daytime and 1,000 people at night, although this number was often exceeded. The shelter was in use from a very early stage. The Grand Secretary, Sydney White, wrote a letter to the President of the Board of General Purposes on 6 September 1939, just three days after war had been declared, to report mainly on the meeting of Grand Lodge that had been held that day. But in his letter he highlighted what was to be one of the continuing problems of all shelters, what he described as 'the atmosphere'. 'I have arranged for the place to be sprayed with disinfectant. I shall have to see if I cannot do something about it but the difficulty is we must not open windows.'

Members of staff became volunteer Shelter Wardens, usually two per night. The Grand Secretary took a great personal interest in the work and he often remained on the premises at night and took his turn in the Shelter Warden duties. Miss Haig, his secretary, and other female members of staff, were responsible for first aid and running the canteen. At Christmas 1940 those using the shelter had a collection amongst themselves, which raised £30, which was spent on decorating the shelter and providing Christmas trees and toys for the children. The Grand Secretary attended a children's tea and the Maintenance Superintendent, Mr Tribe, acted as Father Christmas.

Freemasons' Hall survived without major damage during the bombing raids on London. During the Blitz, at 9.10pm on Saturday, 11 January 1941 bombs fell nearby and the blast broke all the windows on the Wild Street side of the building and some on the Wild Court elevation. Some of the glass cases in the Museum, which is on the Wild Court side of the building, remain pitted from the bomb damage. Freemasons' Hall was converted into a temporary first aid post for the injured and homeless.

Further damage was caused in June 1944 by a flying bomb that landed in Long Acre and caused blast damage to windows and doors.

The Library and Museum was temporarily closed in September 1939 but soon reopened although the china and glass were stored in the basement, the pictures, aprons and furniture moved to a mezzanine floor and the silver and jewels were kept in the safe. Although the blackout meant that the Library and Museum had to be closed rather earlier than usual every day, the Librarian and Curator reported the daily attendance remained comparable with its prewar levels, at least in the early stages of the war, with about 700-800 visitors a month. By 1944 annual visitor numbers of 2,500 were reported (ie about 200 a month) rising to 4,000 in 1945. A steady stream of donations was received. The Librarian and Curator was also responsible for administering the collection of Masonic medals that were melted down for the war effort and raised considerable sums.

One of the major problems facing Grand Lodge was lack of manpower. As well as having to maintain the building and repair occasional damage, there was additional work to do in terms of maintaining the shelter (10 women were employed to clean the shelter every day) and looking after the increased number of lodges meeting in the building. There remained the continuing clerical work of keeping membership registers up to date, issuing certificates, chasing dues and organising the quarterly Grand Lodge meetings, which continued throughout the war. Increasingly manpower resources were concentrated on maintaining the building.

Troops marching along Great Queen Street.

Artefacts from the wartime period.

Great Queen Street after 1945

The combined result of slum clearance, commercial expansion and an increasing institutional demand for property led to a decline in the residential population in the immediate area and this trend was accentuated by the Second World War when the Borough of Holborn lost nearly 15 per cent of its buildings. Great Queen Street was not badly affected by bombing although the theatre at the east end of the street was damaged and some buildings on Kingsway were destroyed.

Commemorative stone marking the 250th anniversary of the first Grand Lodge.

In 1965 local government reorganisation amalgamated the Borough of Holborn with St Pancras and Hampstead to create the London Borough of Camden in the Greater London Council (GLC). This entity remained in place after the abolition of the GLC in 1986.

The major development in the area in the post-war years was on the Covent Garden site. The market closed in 1974. Local councils drew up plans for the site to include a conference centre in the Piazza with elevated pedestrian walkways and new roads which were to include a sunken four-lane carriageway. Wild Street, adjacent to Freemasons' Hall, was to be enlarged as a major thoroughfare. There was considerable local opposition to the plans that resulted in the listing of over 200 buildings in the area and instead an emphasis on protecting established trades and activities. Charles Fowler's market was converted to house restaurants and shops and the Flower Market converted into a museum. The area became a major tourist attraction.

The 18th century Wesleyan Chapel at the eastern end of Great Queen Street had been demolished in 1910 and replaced by an entrance to the Kingsway Hall, the base for the West London Mission of the Methodist Church. This later became a recording venue for classical and film music but following the collapse of part of the roof in the 1970s, it was sold to the GLC. When the GLC was abolished in 1986 the Hall fell into further disrepair and was demolished and the site redeveloped as a hotel in the 1990s. The business character of Great Queen Street changed as the Covent Garden area became more focussed on tourism and leisure.

Although the competition for the Masonic Peace Memorial Building had specified that accommodation should be provided for the RMBI, this was not taken up and shortly before the 1939-1945 war, the RMBI moved into 20 Great Queen Street on the north side. Having purchased a freehold site at 31 Great Queen Street, also on the north side, in 1923, the RMIG commissioned a new building, designed by E. R. Barrow which had been opened in 1926. When the RMIG and the RMIB were amalgamated to form the Masonic Trust for Girls and Boys in the 1980s, the RMIB moved from Puerorum House (26 Great Queen Street) into the RMIG building.

Before and after the 1939-45 War Grand Lodge purchased a number of properties on the north side of the street and in Drury Lane and Parker Street as investment properties. In the years after the Second World War Freemasons' Hall continued to be used for its masonic functions but remained closed to other uses just as Grand Lodge remained largely unresponsive to requests for information about freemasonry. Few changes were made to the building apart from the clock on the tower and a stone plaque that were installed in 1967 to mark the 250th anniversary of the founding of the first Grand Lodge in 1717. Refurbishment of electrical wiring and window frames and a programme of regular redecoration helped to maintain the building to a high standard and in keeping with its Grade 2* listing.

In April 1985, the Grand Master, the Duke of Kent, instituted a more open policy on relations with the public and the press. This was reflected in the opening of the building for public tours and of the Library and Museum for research use by non-members. In July 1986 an exhibition on the historical development of freemasonry opened to the public. This followed the publication in the previous year of the first 'guidebook' to the building, *Freemasons' Hall, the Home and Heritage of the Craft*. In 2002 a series of events

The tower of Freemasons' Hall, showing the clock installed in 1967.

were held in the building to mark the first national *Freemasonry in the Community* week. Once again the building began to be used for non-Masonic events serving as a venue for performances of Mozart and Handel during the Covent Garden Festival. The building has become an important location for films and television programmes and for advertising photography.

Early in 2006 it was announced that the lower ground floor of Freemasons' Hall would be converted into office accommodation to house the four national Masonic charities. In his statement, the President of the Board of General Purposes echoed many of the ideas of his predecessors: 'Better use will be made of the space available in Freemasons' Hall and the other properties in Great Queen Street . . . The Charities… have a common purpose with the Craft. It seems eminently sensible that the various administrations should all be housed under one roof where they can work together for the good of freemasonry in general.' As the present Freemasons' Hall approaches its 75th anniversary, it has established its own history and place in London.

The Covent Garden area as a tourist destination.
Reproduced with the kind permission of In and Around Covent Garden

Programme for the Covent Garden Festival during which musical performances were held at Freemasons' Hall.

Freemasons' Hall: A Photographic Essay

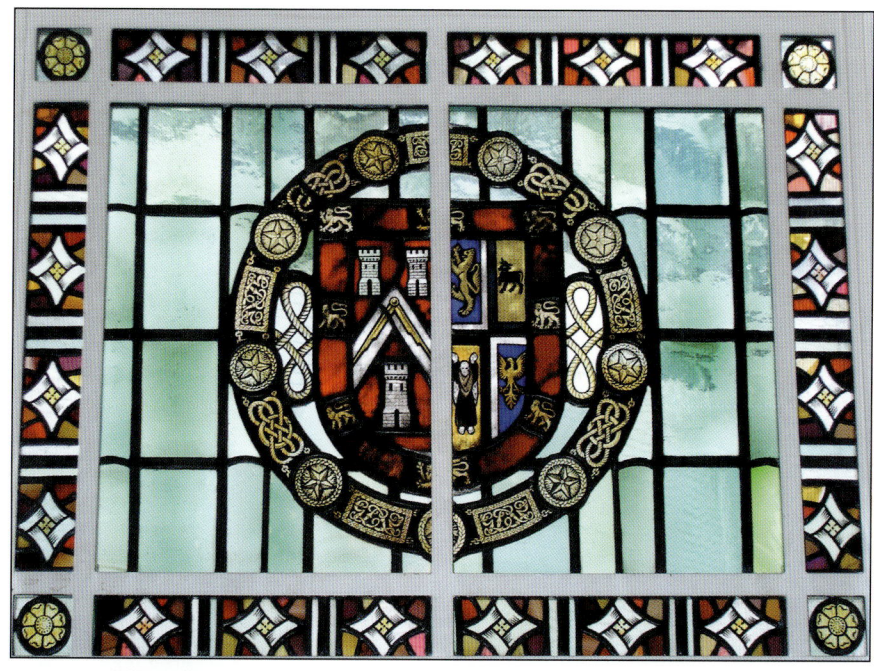

Freemasons' Hall covers a site of over 2 acres with a frontage on Great Queen Street of 450ft (150m) and on Wild Street of 280ft (93m). A modern steel frame construction combined with high-quality materials created a building which, from the everyday lodge rooms to the grandest ceremonial areas and from the largest pieces of furniture down to the smallest detail reflects craftsmanship of the highest quality.

Access to the upper floors is via an elegant staircase leading to a drawing room and the Library and Museum.

The elegance of the building is combined with practicality as the walls of the internal courtyards, one which is shown here (left) are lined with self cleaning ceramic bricks.

George Daniels designed the stained glass panels on the main staircase.

There are over 20 lodge rooms in the building.

There is extensive use of stained glass as a decorative feature throughout the building. In the Processional Corridor, panels depicting the cardinal virtues are by George Kruger Gray (1880-1943) who trained at the Royal College of Art and was influenced by W. R. Lethaby. He was a noted designer of coinage, seals and medals (including the great seal of George VI), using his knowledge of heraldry.

Master's chair in one of the lodge rooms.

A marble clad vestibule, facing west, contains the memorial window and Roll of Honour housed in a bronze casket.

Stained glass memorial window.

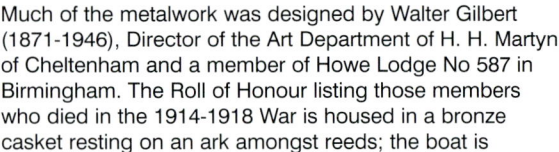

The bronze casket in which the Roll of Honour is displayed.

Much of the metalwork was designed by Walter Gilbert (1871-1946), Director of the Art Department of H. H. Martyn of Cheltenham and a member of Howe Lodge No 587 in Birmingham. The Roll of Honour listing those members who died in the 1914-1918 War is housed in a bronze casket resting on an ark amongst reeds; the boat is indicative of a journey which has come to an end. In the centre of the front panel a relief shows the Hand of God set in a circle in which rests the Soul of Man. Overall the design and ornamentation incorporate symbols connected with the theme of peace and the attainment of eternal life. At the four corners of the Shrine stand pairs of winged Seraphim carrying golden trumpets and across the front are four gilded figures portraying (from left to right) Moses the Law Giver, Joshua the Warrior Priest, Solomon the Wise and St George.

Gilbert also designed the bronze doors which mark the entrance to the Grand Temple. Each door is cast in one piece and weighs 1¼ tons. On the outside of the doors a series of panels represent the story of the building of King Solomon's Temple.

The handles on the inside of the doors are made by the hilts of the swords with their points embedded, indicating that they are not in use, that this is a peace memorial.

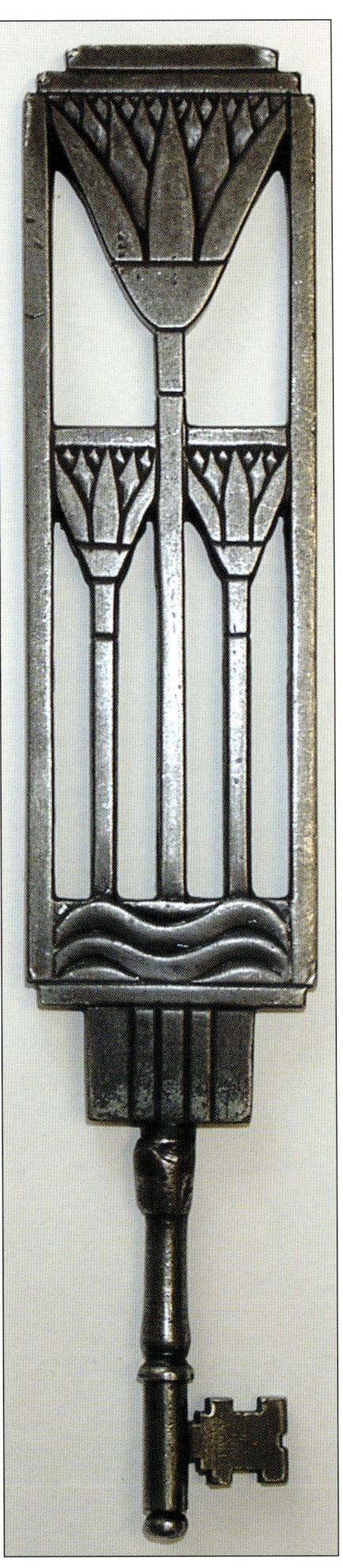

The doors to the Grand Temple had their own special key.

The Grand Master's throne, made for the Grand Temple in 1933.

The stained glass in the Grand Temple represents the rays of the sun.

The frieze on the walls over the side doors of the Grand Temple is decorated in gilt with the signs of the zodiac — a homage to the ceiling design of Thomas Sandby's Hall.

The decoration of the cornice, which is 15ft deep, is entirely in mosaic. The allegorical groups in the design each incorporate columns of a Classical order of architecture. On the eastern side of the cornice, between two Ionic pillars (representing Wisdom), is shown a representation of the Ark of the Covenant and Jacob's Ladder. Resting against the Ladder is the Volume of Sacred Law (any holy book displayed at a lodge meeting). Jacob's Ladder bears the symbols for Faith (a cross), Hope (an anchor) and Charity (a burning heart), ascending towards the Hebrew character of YOD (Jehovah). To the left stands King Solomon, to the right King Hiram, the builders of the first Temple at Jerusalem.

On the western side are two Doric pillars (representing strength of knowledge) flanked by Euclid and Pythagoras on either side of the 47th Proposition of Euclid (the symbol worn by a Past Master of a Lodge). The pillars support the Moon, around which is an ancient symbol of wisdom, the serpent.

On the northern side, between the two pillars of the Composite order, are the arms of the Duke of Connaught and Strathearn (Grand Master when this Hall was built). On one side is St George and on the other the Dragon. The celestial globe on one pillar and the terrestrial globe on the other represent the universal nature of freemasonry. At the base of the pillars are two blocks of stone (ashlars). One is rough, representing Man entering freemasonry, and the other is smooth, representing how Man is improved through freemasonry.

On the southern side are two Corinthian pillars (representing beauty) with Helios, the Sun God, driving his chariot across the heavens to mark the Sun at its meridian. The pillars support the All-Seeing Eye, below which is a five-pointed star.

In contrast to the historical theme on the other side, the inner face of the Grand Temple Doors is decorated with symbolic figures beneath the starry girdle of heaven and the hands of a Supreme Being weighing the Soul of Man (right).

Amongst the figures are Labour, holding a two handled saw, (right) and Wisdom in Council (far right).

Evocotive of the 1914–1918 War, this pair of soldiers (above) represent duty and self sacrifice. Hiram Abiff (left), architect of Solomon's Temple and representing beauty here holds his plan of the The Temple.

Notes on Sources

The history of the development of the Great Queen Street site can be traced in the minutes of the *Quarterly Communication of* Grand Lodge (and the Premier Grand Lodge before 1813), in the Hall Committee minutes and other archive and library material held at the Library and Museum of Freemasonry in London. A leaflet called *Exploring Masonic Records: Freemasons' Hall and Tavern* gives more information about the archive material available. The Library and Museum catalogue is available online at www.freemasonry.london.museum

For further detail on the history of the buildings in Great Queen Street see Camden History Society *Streets of St Giles*, London, 2000, and London County Council *Survey of London Volume V: the Parish of St Giles-in-the-Fields (Part II)*, London, 1914.

There are a number of useful articles in the Transactions of the leading English Masonic research lodge, *Ars Quatuor Coronatorum (AQC)*, including the following:

Douglas Burford, 'The Ark of the Masonic Covenant' in *AQC*, Volume 105, London, 1993

Terence O. Haunch, 'The Freemasons' Hall Medal of 1780' in *AQC*, Volume 82, London, 1969

Sir James Stubbs, 'Major Portraits at Freemasons' Hall, London', *AQC*, Volume 79, London, 1966

Sir James Stubbs, 'Great Queen Street — Freemasons' Hall & its Environs', *AQC*, Volume 81, London, 1968

Aspects of the story can be explored further in the following:

Rebecca Coombes, *Guardians of the past, keepers for the future: the role of the Librarian and Curator at the United Grand Lodge of England*, Library and Museum of Freemasonry, London, 1999

Terence Gerard Galvin, *The Architecture of Joseph Michael Gandy (1771-1843) and Sir John Soane (1753-1837): An Exploration into the Masonic and Occult Imagination of the late Enlightenment*, PhD dissertation, University of Pennsylvania, 2003

John M. Hamill, 'And the Greatest of these is Charity': the Development of Masonic Charity, Prestonian Lecture, London, 1993

Gordon P. G. Hills, *The Grand Lodge Library and Museum*, Library and Museum of Freemasonry, London, c1932

Bryan Page, *A history of the Library and Museum of Freemasonry*, Ms, London, 2004

Sir James Stubbs and Terence O. Haunch, *Freemasons' Hall: the Home and Heritage of the Craft*, London, 1983

David Watkin, 'Freemasonry and Sir John Soane', in *JSAH*, Volume 54, December 1995